Jackson Wayne

An Introduction to the Biblical Worldview and Contemporary Moral Issues

RLGN 105

Fourth Edition

Dr. Lew A. Weider
Liberty University

An Introduction to the Biblical Worldview and Contemporary Moral Issues, Fourth Edition
RLGN 105

Copyright © 2022 by Lew A. Weider

Scripture taken from the Holy Bible, King James Version, New Living Translation, New International Version.

All rights reserved. No part of this publication may be reproduced or transmitted in any form or by any means, electronic or mechanical, including photocopying, recording, or any information storage and retrieval system, without the written permission of the publisher.

Requests for permission to make copies of any part of the work should be mailed to:

Permissions Department
Academx Publishing Services, Inc.
P.O. Box 208
Sagamore Beach, MA 02562
http://www.academx.com

Printed in the United States of America

ISBN-13: 978-1-68284-920-0
ISBN-10: 1-68284-920-1

TABLE OF CONTENTS

Becoming a Critical Thinker

Chapter 1 - Critical Thinking 1

Developing a Biblical/Christian Worldview

Chapter 2 - Understanding Worldview 9

Chapter 3 - A Biblical Worldview 15

Chapter 4 - Developing a Biblical Ethic 19

Chapter 5 - Christian Liberty 25

Contemporary Religious Worldviews

Chapter 6 - Religious Worldviews 29

Tolerance and the Biblical/Christian Worldview

Chapter 7 - Tolerance 45

Biblical Worldview Application

Chapter 8 - Abortion 49

Chapter 9 - Euthanasia 57

Chapter 10 - Gender Issues 63

Chapter 11 - Homosexuality 71

Chapter 12 - Relationships 77

Chapter 13 - Racism 83

Chapter 14 - Poverty 89

Biblical Worldview and Contemporary Issues Resource List 97

Chapter 1: Critical Thinking

Chapter Overview:

Love Your God with All Your Mind: J.P. Moreland

Admonition from Scripture

What is Critical Thinking?

Characteristics of Critical Thinking

Why should you Care?

Notable Terms

Informal Logical Fallacies

"We must be willing to seek the truth in a spirit of humility with an admission of our own finitude, we must be willing to learn from our critics, and we need to learn to argue against our own positions in order to strengthen our understanding of them."

J.P Moreland, *Love Your God with All Your Mind*, (Navpress, 2012), p.125.

"An educated person is expected to have some understanding of, and experience in thinking about moral and ethical problems. It may well be that the most significant quality in educated persons is the informed judgement which enables them to make discriminating moral choices."

Harvard's Report on the *"Core Curriculum"* in The Chronicle of Higher Education (March 6, 1978), p.15.

The Thinker by Augustus Rodin. The Musee Rodin Paris, France.

ADMONITION FROM SCRIPTURE

Proverbs 14:15 (NIV) *"A simple man believes anything, but a prudent man gives thought to his steps."*
Acts 17:11 (NLT) *"And the people of Berea were more open minded than those in Thessalonica, and they listened eagerly to Paul's message. They searched the Scriptures day after day to check up on Paul and Silas, to see if they were really teaching the truth."*
Colossians 2:8 (NLT) *"Don't let anyone lead you astray with empty philosophy and high-sounding nonsense that come from human thinking and from the evil powers of this world, and not from Christ."*
1 Thessalonians 5:21 (ESV) *"But test everything, hold fast to what is good."*
1 Peter 3:15 (NIV) *"But in your hearts set apart Christ as Lord. Always be prepared to give an answer to everyone who asks you to give the reason for the hope that you have. But do this with gentleness and respect."*

I. What is Critical Thinking?
  A. It is recognizing and evaluating *opinion* and so called *evidence*.
  B. It is reflecting on the meaning and significance of statements and ideas.
  C. It test the *validity?* of statements and ideas.

"Wait – Isn't Critical Thinking Secular?"

"Some Christians may be concerned because critical thinking is a concept praised by secularists who promote 'rationality'. The word rational means having reason or being reasonable. Critical thinking is rational in the sense that it involves logical reasoning. Secularists, however, may try to incorrectly redefine rational as "excluding God." This doesn't mean critical thinking is secular, just that the definition of rational has been manipulated.

Ironically, however, a biblical worldview— not a secular one—provides the foundation for logic, making critical thinking possible. We can think critically because God is the source of absolutes. He created a logical universe and gave us faculties for reasoning. Unlike messages that contradict the Bible, God's Word will always stand up to scrutiny. Ultimately, Christians have no reason to resist critical thinking and every reason to embrace it." Engler, Patricia (2021). *Tools for Critical Thinking.* https://answersingenesis.org/apologetics/tools-critical-thinking/

II. What are Characteristics of Critical Thinkers?
  A. They constantly evaluate their own *actions*, *value* and *opinions*.
  B. They do not pretend to know what they do not know.

C. They do not blindly adhere to **tradition**.
D. They resist and refuse to use manipulation.
E. They seek **clarification of terms**
F. They explore many sides of an issue.
G. They base their opinions and judgments on **evidence**
H. They are eager to learn from the experience of others.
I. They look for **fallacies** in the arguments of others.

III. Why should You Care about Critical Thinking?

A. It helps you to make sense of life and the world around you.
B. It helps you to do your job more effectively.
C. It helps you to avoid being ripped off.
D. It helps you to prepare for everyday life
   1. Are these statistics true?
   2. Why are they mad at me?
   3. How should I prepare for this storm? Evacuate?
   4. Why should I marry this person?
   5. What are my chances of winning the lottery?
   6. Is this story true?

IV. Notable Terms Related to Critical Thinking

A. **Opinion** - A belief or conclusion about reality. Unlike facts, opinions are open to question and analysis by critical thinking.

B. **Argument** - In the formal sense, arguments attempt to offer evidence to demonstrate the reasonableness of an opinion. Arguments can be sound (logical) or unsound (dependent upon logical fallacies). There are two parts of a good argument.

   1. **Evidence** - The basis or cause of a belief. It is a statement or justification, an explanation of a belief or action.
   2. **Conclusion** - A decision based upon reasoning, deduction, or inference.

C. **The Law of** _Non-Contradiction_

Definition: Something cannot both exist and not exist or be true and false at the same time and in the say way.

D. **Logical Fallacies**

In rhetoric, a fallacy is simply any error, whether intentional or unintentional, in reasoning. (The most common kinds of fallacies of logic are Informal and are the ones students really need to familiarize themselves with. Think of them as counterfeit arguments.)

INFORMAL LOGICAL FALLACIES YOU SHOULD KNOW

1. Oversimplification	Concluding that an effect has only one cause when it is really the result of multiple causes.
2. Hasty Conclusion	Making a judgement on the basis of one or even a few samples.
3. Overgeneralization	(Stereotyping) making a judgement about an entire group based on behavior, mostly undesirable, of a few from that group.
4. False Analogies	Arguing on the basis of a comparison of unrelated things.
5. Slippery Slope	Arguing against an action on the unsupported assertion that it will inevitably lead to a much worse condition.
6. Sweeping Generalization	Stating a general principle and then applying it in a specific case as though it were a universal rule.
7. Ad Hominem	(Lit. "To the man") Seeking to discredit a person's argument by attacking their personal character, origin, associations, etc.
8. Appeal to Authority	Appealing to the opinion of a person who agrees with yours because they are generally respected by the audience, but have no real authority on the topic at hand.

#	Term	Definition
9.	Appeal to ignorance	Claiming that something is true simply because it cannot be disproved, or that something is untrue because it cannot be proved.
10.	Bandwagon	Justifying a course of action because everyone is doing it.
11.	Is/Ought or naturalistic fallacy	Concluding about the way things ought to be simply on the basis of how things are or are assumed to be.
12.	Selective Perception	Looking only for things that support our current ideas, and ignoring evidence that does not.
13.	False Dilemma	Oversimplifying a complex issue to make it appear that only two alternatives are possible.
14.	Red Herring	Raising an irrelevant issue to divert attention from the primary issue. This argument appeals to a person's fears or sense of pity.
15.	Straw Man	Misrepresenting a position to make it seem weaker than it really is or to demonize the position to make it sound worse than it is and then to act as if the argument has been won when the real issue hasn't even been addressed.
16.	Genetic Fallacy	Giving credit to a position or supporting a claim because of the origin (genesis) of the position when such an appeal to origin is irrelevant.

INFORMAL LOGICAL FALLACIES – EXAMPLE SHEET

(For practice identify the fallacies. The answers are at the bottom of the page.)

1. Argument: _____

"Did you hear about that illegal alien from Mexico who shot and killed that guy in California. You can trust any of them and they should all be shipped back to Mexico".

2. Argument: _____

"Everyone ought to be drinking Green Tea. The Chinese drink it all the time and they do not have near the incidents of heart disease that we do in the U.S. Further, most Chinese men live at least twenty more years than the average American male."

3. Argument: _____

"Here is my opponent, speaking to you of the value of all human life. She believes that human life begins at conception and should be legally protected. But she can't be trusted. She even admitted she had an abortion when she was a teenager!"

4. Argument: _____

"How can you speak out against the fact that 6 million Jews were killed during the Holocaust, but you say nothing about the 600 million chickens killed every year just to satisfy your hunger for meat?"

5. Argument: _____

"Hanes must be the best underwear on the market. Michael Jordan wouldn't wear anything but the best."

6. Argument: _____

"I know that God exists because no one has ever provided evidence on the contrary."

7. Argument: _____

"I can't believe that Liberty University allows kissing on campus. The next thing you know they will start to allow co-ed dorms and eventually abandon its Christian principles."

8. Argument: _____

"Because humans act basically on self-interest and are selfish by nature, we should always and only do that which is our best interest."

9. Argument: _____

Candidate A: "Although the Constitution does not define the term 'person' science tells us that the unborn are human and should be protected by law."

Candidate B: "Well, if the law were changed as my opponent desires and if abortion became 'illegal except to save the woman's life in my state, women would resort to back-alley abortions again, which are very unsafe and often deadly."

10. Argument: _____

"Mom, can I get my belly-button pierced? Everyone at school is getting one."

11. Argument: _____

"Transgender rights are the issues of greatest importance at this time in our nation. It's the last oppression. The US must take this step in ending oppression, just like it did when it outlawed slavery and established civil rights for its black citizens."

12. Argument: _____

"Affirmative action means one thing, injustice. As we continue to set quotas that keep qualified white males from getting jobs, we are promoting reverse discrimination. Face, it; if you are not against affirmative action, you are for injustice."

13. Argument: _____

"She will never make it in college. She made C's and D's in High School."

14. Argument: _____

"As Americans, we believe in the 'freedom of the press' therefore, reporters should not be hindered from reporting our troop's movements in the war zone."

15. Argument: _____

"People who are against abortion like you have no respect for women's rights. You think women want to get pregnant just to abort the child. That's ridiculous. Women must have the right to choose whether they want a baby or not."

16. Argument: _____

Jenny: "Mom, Tommy told me that God doesn't exist."
Mom: "Jenny, I have always told you that God exists and I believe He does exist."
Jenny: "Tommy, you're wrong. My mom said so."

"You can't believe anything the news reports. It's all fake news".

Answers:

1. Overgeneralization/ Stereotyping	2. Oversimplification	3. Ad Hominem
4. False Analogy	5. Appeal to False Authority	6. Appeal to Ignorance
7. Slippery Slope	8. Is/Ought-Naturalistic Fallacy	9. Red Herring
10. Bandwagon	11. False Analogy	12. False Dilemma
13. Hasty Conclusion	14. Sweeping Generalization	15. Straw Man
16. Genetic Fallacy		

Chapter 2:
Understanding Worldview

Chapter Overview:

A Call to Resist the Secular Assault on Mind, Morals, and Meaning: Nancy Pearcey

Admonition from Scripture

What a Worldview is not

What is a Worldview?

Five Questions to Understanding Worldview

Differing Worldviews

Secular Ideologies

Valid Worldview

"Christians are paying the price for adopting the fortress mentality over the past century and not paying attention to the questions people are asking. A better approach was suggested by C. S. Lewis when he said that in every subject area, it is Christians who should think the most deeply and be the most creative."

Nancy Pearcy, Saving Leonardo: A Call to Resist the Secular Assault on Mind, Morals, and Meaning. (Nashville, Tennessee: B & H Publishing Group 2010, p.254.

ADMONITION FROM SCRIPTURE

Genesis 1:1 (KJV) – *"In the beginning God created the heaven and the earth."*

Genesis 1:26-27 (NIV) *"So God created mankind in his own image, in the image of God he created them; male and female he created them".*

Romans 12:1-2 (NIV) – *"Therefore, I urge you, brothers, in view of God's mercy, to offer your bodies as living sacrifices, holy and pleasing to God – this is your spiritual act of worship. Do not conform any longer to the pattern of this world but be transformed by the renewing of your mind. Then you will be able to test and approve what God's will is – his good, pleasing and perfect will."*

Acts 28:1-6 - *(Notice the reaction of the people based upon their worldview.)*

QUESTIONS

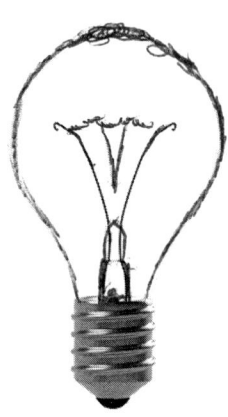

- What is Epistemology and why is it important?
- What is a Worldview?
- Do I have a Worldview?
- What is my Worldview?
- How can I have a consistent Worldview?

I. What A Worldview is Not.

A. It is not just a person's __perception__ of the world. i.e., "I think this world is in trouble because it has so many problems like poverty, disease, genocide and something needs to be done about it."

Note: Our perception or opinion is not our worldview, but rather it is the result of our worldview.

B. It is not limited to those who study __Philosophy__ or religion.
No one should say, "I don't have a worldview." That is not to say that everyone has a well-established worldview and operates consistently within its framework.

II. What is a Worldview?

A. "A worldview is a commitment, a fundamental orientation of the heart, that can be expressed as a story or in a set of presuppositions (assumptions which may be true, partially true or entirely false) that we hold (consciously or subconsciously, consistently or inconsistently) about the basic constitution of reality, and that provides the foundation on which we live and move and have our being."
James W. Sire, *The Universe Next Door*, (Intervarsity, 2009).

B. It is the basis for your moral __decision making__.

C. "It is simply the sum total of our beliefs about the world, the 'big picture' that directs our daily decisions and actions."
Charles Colson & Nancy Pearcey, *How Shall We Live* (Tyndale House, 1999).

D. It's like looking through colored glasses or lenses. What we see is impacted by the tint of the lens.

E. "A worldview, whether Christian or secular, is the unifying perspective from which we organize our thinking about life, death, art, science, faith learning, work, money, values, and morals. A worldview is our underlying philosophy of life."
Ken Hemphill, *Life Answers*, (Lifeway Press, 1993)

QUESTIONS

➢ What are some external forces that can influence our worldview?
➢ Why does a person's worldview matter? Because it impacts what they do.

III. To A Worldview One Must Ask At Least These Five Questions Understand.

A. The question of __Origin__ - *"How did life begin in the first place?" "Where did humans get here?"*

B. The question of __identity__ - *"What does it mean to be human?" "Am I more important than animals?"*

C. The question of __Meaning__ (purpose) – *"Why are we here?" "Why am I here?"*

D. The question of __Morality__ (ethics) – *"What is meant by right and wrong?" "How should I live?"*

E. The question of __destiny__ - *"Is there life after death?" "What will happen to me when I die?" "Will I have to answer for the choices I made and how I lived my life?"*

IV. Three Major Claims of Differing Worldviews

A. __Naturalism__ - The only reality exists in the natural realm

Examples: *Secular Humanism* – Man is the central focus of decision making.
Atheism – God does not exist.

B. __Pantheism__ - God and the world are the same thing.

Examples: *Eastern Religious, Christian Science, The New Age Movement, etc.*

C. __Theism__ - God exists, was the creator of the world, and is personally and intimately involved with his creation. God operates through natural law but can and does intervene in the affairs of mankind.

Examples: *Judaism, Christianity, and Islam.*

V. America's Secular Ideologies

Societies also reflect their own worldview(s).

Here in America for example the dominant ideologies that pervade our society would include materialism, subjectivism, hedonism, and pragmatism.

A. __Materialism__.
  - Philosophical Concept: Reality is based in which we can "know"
  - Social Application: Absolute truth is non-existent or irrelevant to society. Mankind seeks satisfaction and meaning in external things such as position, wealth, accomplishments, etc. The only things that exist are in the material world.

B. __Subjectivism__:
  - Philosophical Concept: There is no Truth
  - Social Application: "Everyone is entitled to their opinion." Feelings become authoritative! Individuals make moral choices based upon what makes them happy. Moral and social chaos ensues, for there are no absolutes of right and wrong.

C. __Hedonism__ : Intellectual/sensual
   - Philosophical Concept:
   - Social Application: *The pursuit of pleasure, comfort, safety and security is the highest good. Struggle and pain are defined as evil. The highest good is intellectual or physical pleasure. "If it feels good, do it!"*

D. __Pragmatism__ :
   - Philosophical Concept: the ends justifies the means
   - Social Application: The key concept is doing what works or is practical. Focus is upon intentions rather than upon right and wrong. If one's "intentions" are good, it does not matter what they do. It can be an individual or societal approach to morality.

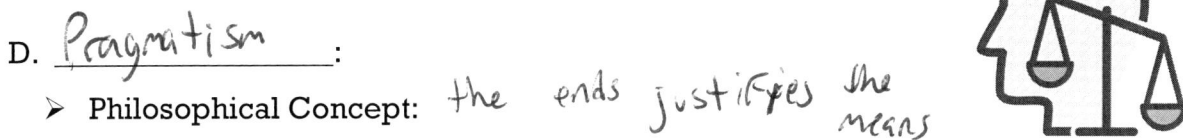

VI. Three Criteria for Determining A Valid Worldview

A. __Coherence__ - My answers to the above questions must be consistent with one another; i.e. they must not contradict each other.
Example: The questions of origin and identity.

B. __Adequacy__ - My answers must deal truthfully and completely with all the facts it encounters.
Example: The Anthropic Principle

C. __Relevance__ - My worldview must make sense of the emotions and feelings I have as I interact with the world around me.
Example: Why do I feel guilt, sadness, joy, etc.?

Chapter 3:
A Biblical Worldview

Chapter Overview:

Mere Christianity: C.S Lewis

Admonition from Scripture

Biblical Worldview

Basic Concepts

Biblical Metanarrative

6 Reasons why we need a Worldview

R.C Sproul

"You must make your choice: either this man was, and is, the Son of God, or else a madman or something worse. You can shut him up for a fool, you can spit at him and kill him as a demon; or you can fall at his feet and call him Lord and God."

Lewis, C.S., Mere Christianity, London: Collins, 1952, pp.54-56. (In all editions, this is Bk.II, Ch.3, and "The Shocking Alternative.")

"As with every aspect of our sanctification, the renewal of the mind may be painful and difficult. It requires hard work and discipline, inspired by a sacrificial love for Christ and a burning desire to build up His Body, the Church. Developing a Christian worldview means submitting our entire self to God, in an act of devotion and service to Him."

Pearcy, N. (2008). Total Truth: Liberating Christianity From its Cultural Captivity. Wheaton, III: Crossway Books.

ADMONITION FROM SCRIPTURE

> **I Peter 3:15 (NKJV)** *"But in your hearts revere Christ as Lord. Always be prepared to give an answer to everyone who asks you to give the reason for the hope that you have. But do this with gentleness and respect."*

> **II Timothy 2:15 (NIV)** *"Do your best to present yourself to God as one approved, a worker who does not need to be ashamed and who correctly handles the word of truth."*

> **Philippians 4:8-9 (NKJV)** *"Finally, brethren, whatever things are true, whatever things are noble, whatever things are just, whatever things are pure, whatever things are lovely, whatever things are of good report, if there is any virtue and if there is anything praise worthy-meditate of these things. The things which you learned and received and heard and saw in me, these do, and the God of peace will be with you."*

I. **Questions to Consider**
   A. Do I think Biblically?
   B. Do I make my daily decisions from a Biblical and Christian framework? What does that look like on a daily basis?
   C. How can I apply the Biblical/Christian Worldview to my family, my relationships, and my career?

II. **How the Biblical Worldview Answers the Five Key Questions**
   A. Origin – God created the heavens, earth, and all living things (Genesis 1:1; 2:21-25; Colossians 1:16).
   B. Identity – God created humans uniquely in His image. Humans are more important that other living things (Genesis 1:26-27).
   C. Meaning or Purpose – God has a purpose for all humanity (John 17:3; I Corinthians 10:31).
   D. Morality – The Bible is humanity's guide to right and wrong thoughts, motives, and actions (Psalm 119:11; II Timothy 3:16-17).
   E. Destiny – Humans will spend eternity in heaven or hell based upon their relationship with Jesus Christ (John 1:11-13; John 3:16).

III. **The Basic Concepts of the Biblical Worldview**
   A. ___God exists___ - (Genesis 1:1)
   B. God has revealed ___Himself___ to mankind – (Hebrews 1:1-2)
   C. ___Jesus Christ___ is God's Son who is redeemer of the world (John 3:16)
   D. The Bible is God's ___Word___ - (II Timothy 3:16; I Peter 1:21).
   E. Christians are to follow the teachings of the ___Bible___ (II Timothy 3:16-17; John 14:15)

IV. A Biblical/Christian Worldview Metanarrative

A Metanarrative is an all-encompassing story or storyline that give context, meaning, and purpose to all of life. A Biblical metanarrative describes the story of God from Genesis to Revelation showing how God has worked throughout history for an ultimate purpose of humanity's restoration to God Himself.
  A. Creation – God has revealed Himself (Hebrews 1:1-2)
  B. Fall – Humanity (Adam and Eve) chose to disobey God and sin. (Genesis 3; Romans 5:12)
  C. Redemption – God's story of redemption is through the remainder of The Bible in both the Old and New Testaments. (Romans 5:8)

V. Six Reasons Why We Need a Worldview Based Upon God's Word.
  A. It helps us integrate biblical principles with daily life.
  B. It provides a foundation for and gives substance to our faith. "Why do you call me, 'Lord, Lord,' and do not do what I say? As for everyone who comes to me and hears my words and puts them into practice, I will show you what they are like. They are like a man building a house, who dug down deep and laid the foundation on rock. When a flood came, the torrent struck that house but could not shake it, because it was well built. But the one who hears my words and does not put them into practice is like a man who built a house on the ground without a foundation. The moment the torrent struck that house, it collapsed and its destruction was complete." (Luke 6:46-49)
  C. It is essential because of an overt challenge from the secular world. "Then we will no longer be infants, tossed back and forth by the waves, and blown here and there by every wind of teaching and by the cunning and craftiness of people in their deceitful scheming." (Ephesians 4:14)
  D. It gives us a more effective witness. "But in your hearts revere Christ as Lord. Always be prepared to give an answer to everyone who asks you to give the reason for the hope that you have. But do this with gentleness and respect," (I Peter 3:15)
  E. It is essential because the world has become our neighbors. "He must hold firmly to the trustworthy message as it has been taught, so that he can encourage others by sound doctrine and refute those who oppose it." (Titus 1:9)
  F. It is commanded in scripture. "So then, just as you received Christ Jesus as Lord, continue to live your lives in him, rooted and built up in him, strengthened in the faith as you were taught, and overflowing with thankfulness." (Colossians 2:6-7)

Worldview – R.C Sproul (video)

As you view the video, answer the following:

1. What is a worldview?
   _____
   _____

2. Every worldview is a system. Every system should be three things.
   A.
   B.
   C.

3. What are the two ultimate divisions of worldviews?
   A.
   B.
   C.

4. Define:
   A. Theocentric –
   B. Anthropocentric –
   C. Syncretism –

5. What is Nihilism –

6. What did R.C. Sproul use to illustrate Nihilism? _____

Chapter 4: Developing a Biblical Ethic

"…..ethics as such is interested less in what people in fact do than in what they ought to do, less in what values presently are and more in what their values out to be."

Arthur F. Holmes, Ethics – Approaching Moral Decisions, Intervarsity Press, 1984, p.2.

"Ethics are important because moral questions are at the heart of life's most important issues. Morality is primarily concerned with questions of right and wrong, the ability to distinguish between the two, and the justification for the distinction…..You cannot formulate an adequate worldview without providing answers to these moral questions."

-Scott Rae, Moral Choices: Introduction to Ethics, Zondervan Press, 1995, p.12.

Chapter Overview:

Ethics- Approaching Moral Decisions Arthur F. Holmes

Admonition from Scripture

Essentialism

The Revelation of the Good and Right

What is so special about the Word of God?

Characteristics of a Biblical Ethic

Absolutism

Moral Crises

Case Studies

ADMONITION FROM SCRIPTURE

> **II Timothy 3:16-17 (NLT)** *"All Scripture is inspired by God and is useful to teach us what is true and to make us realize what is wrong in our lives. It straightens us out and teaches us to do what is right. It is God's way of preparing us in every way; fully equipped for every good thing God wants us to do."*

> **Romans 2:14-15** *"Even when Gentiles, who do not have God's written law, instinctively follow what the law says, they show that in their hearts they know right from wrong. They demonstrate that God's law is written within them, for their own consciences either accuse them or tell them they are doing what is right."*

I. The __Origin__ of the Good and Right.

QUESTION

Where does the idea of right originate?

Consider Euthyphro's Dilemma.

ANSWER

What is right ultimately originates in the Unchanging character of God.

PLATO – The Euthyphro Dilemma

Is something right because the gods will it?

Or

Do the gods will it because it is right?

-Essentialism

A. God is __unchanging__ in His essential nature. Malachi 3:6
B. God's essential nature is perfect __holiness__ and __love__. Isaiah 6:3;
C. I John 4:8.
D. Whatever __God wills__ flows from His __nature__. Psalm 145:17
E. Essentialism – the root word is "essence". What is good and right flows from the "essence" or fundamental nature of God.

God's Unchanging DNA

D- __Divinity__
N- __Nature__
A- __Attributes__

II. The **Revelation** of the Good and Right

➢ Question – How do we come to know the right?
➢ Answer –

A. _Natural/General Revelation_ - (Psalm 19:1-6)
   ➢ In a general way God has revealed, and continues to reveal, His moral will to all mankind.

   We see this evidenced in Man – God's creation which has been given moral aptitude.
   1. Our _Conduct_ -Romans 2:14
   2. Our _Conscience_ - Romans 2:15

Conscience: That inward faculty, possessed by all of us which, pronounces judgment upon our attitudes and actions as being either right or wrong, and prompts us to do right.

   3. Our _Conflicts_
   4. Our _Codes_

B. _Special Revelation_ - (Psalm 19:7-11)
   ➢ God makes known vital truths about Himself which He has not made known in nature.

What are examples of "Special Revelation"?

➢ Dreams and visions (Genesis 20:3-7, 28:10-15)
➢ God's Voice (Genesis 22:11: John 12:28)
➢ OT appearances of Christ (Genesis 18:1-8: Daniel 3:25)
➢ God's Word (II Timothy 3:16, II Peter 1:21)

What is so special about the Word of God?

A. Its _Necessity_
   1. Because of the limits of general revelation.
   2. Because mankind needs a final authority for creed and conduct.

B. Its _Nature_
   1. It is inspired by God.
   2. Through it God reveals specialized truth about Himself.

C. Its _Purpose_
   1. To provide an absolute basis of knowledge concerning the right. II Timothy 3:16
   2. To change our lives. II Timothy 3:17; Ephesians 5:26,27; John 17:17

D. Its Use
   1. Abuses of Scripture
      ➢ **Legalism** – Adding requirements for salvation beyond faith and repentance. Making human preferences necessary for salvation or holy living, which are not specifically required by scripture.
      ➢ **Proof-texting** – Taking scripture out of context to support a personal interpretation.
      ➢ **Denial of inerrancy** – Denying that the Bible is without error in its original manuscripts and cannot be trusted today.
      ➢ **Not recognizing its authority** - When Christians so not use the Bible as their source for divine truth and moral authority.
   2. Its Proper Use
      ➢ _Discerning Principles_ - general, non-changing, descriptive truths about God, man, and all creation.
      ➢ _Discovering Precepts_ - prescriptive truth intended to be a standard or rule, which governs human conduct.
      ➢ _Developing Policies_ - rules/standards of conduct, which are not specifically addressed in Scripture but are derived from its descriptive and prescriptive truth.

III. General Characteristics of a Biblical Ethic
   A. It is based on God's _unchanging nature_.
   B. It is dependent upon God's _revealed truth_.
   C. It is _authoritative_ - It is God "breathed" (inspiration)
   D. It is _prescriptive_ - It tells us how we should live.
   E. It originates from _theological_ and _moral_ absolutes.

IV. Absolutism

A. **What is an Absolute?**
   ➢ Free from imperfection or lack: whole entire, the absolute truth.
   ➢ With no limits or restrictions: absolute power.
   ➢ Absolutely – completely, entirely, without doubt, certainly.

B. **Absolutism versus Relativism**
   Absolute Truth –
   Something that is true at all times and at all places. "Truth is true _at all times and all places_. Truth is discovered or it is revealed, it is not invented by a culture or by religious men."
   Relative Truth –
   "Something that is true to some people and _not to others_. It's true now but it may not have been true in the past and it may not be again in the future, it is _always subject to change_." It is also subject to the perspectives of people. (*Taken from Absolutism versus Relativism* http://www.letusreason.org/Apolo1.htm, 2005)

C. **Perspectives about Absolutes**
   ➢ Norman Geisler – "Since God's moral character does not change, it follows that moral obligations flowing from His nature are absolute."
   (Norman Geisler, *Christian Ethics*, Baker, 2000)

   ➢ Jean Paul Sartre – (French Philosopher) because we see absolutes conflicting there must not be absolutes.

   ➢ Joseph Fletcher – "Situational Ethics" "The ruling norm of Christian decision is love: nothing else." (*Situation Ethics*, The Westminster Press, 1966)

D. **Types of Absolutes**
   ➢ _Theological_ Absolutes – An absolute truth regarding the nature or existence of God and His revelation to mankind.
   ➢ _Moral_ Absolutes – An absolute statement about what is right and wrong, good or evil.

E. **What is Moral Absolutism?**
   ➢ The belief that there is a fixed standard by which moral questions can be answered and moral actions are judged to be right or wrong.
   ➢ The standard determines that certain actions are right or wrong regardless of the circumstances.

V. Categories of Moral Crises

Moral Dilemma- A person experiences a moral dilemma when one must choose between two options, but either option would be wrong to do when taking it on its own.

1.	It is a very rare occurrence.
2.	It is not choosing the lesser of two evil.
3.	It is choosing the greater good. Biblical teaching/examples: Matthew 27:37-39; Matthew 23:23; Romans 13:1-2; Acts 4:19; Acts 5:29.

A. **Crisis of** _Knowledge_ - A seemingly difficult situation which may at first appear to be a moral dilemma, but, in fact, simply requires further information to simplify the decision.
B. **Crisis of** _Conscience_ - A situation in which you know the right thing to do, but sinful nature tempts you to take the easy way out. It is not a dilemma; it is a question of obedience.
C. **Crisis of** _Absolutes_ - A true moral dilemma. Cases and situations in which the right thing to do is difficult to identify because absolute moral duties at least appear to be in conflict. (Clark and Rakestraw, *Readings in Christian Ethics*, Baker, 1994)

VI. **Three Case Studies.**
  A. Is it ever right to _Lie_?
  B. Is it ever right to disobey _Authority_?
  C. Is it ever right to take a _Life_?

Is it ever right to lie? What about deception?

Three types of lying or deception:

➢ Not Sin –

➢ Clearly Sin-

➢ Moral Dilemmas-

Is it ever right to _Disobey Authority_?

➢ Parents?

➢ Government?

➢ School/ Work?

Is it ever right to take a _Take a Life_?

"You shall not murder" –Deuteronomy 5:17

➢ Capital Punishment?

➢ War?

➢ Self Defense?

Make God's Word Your "Moral Compass"

24

Chapter 5:
Christian Liberty

Chapter Overview:

The Works of Jonathan Edwards: J. Edwards

Admonition from Scripture

Essential Definitions

Principles

Guidelines

Summary

"…..in the service of God there is full and free liberty to seek as much pleasure as we please, to enjoy the best kind of pleasure in the world, and as much of it as we possibly can obtain with all our might and main."

Jonathan Edwards, "Christian Liberty", The work of Jonathan Edwards vol.10: Sermons and Discourses 1720-1723 (New Haven: Yale, 1992), 627-628.

ADMONITION FROM SCRIPTURE

> **Romans 14:1-3 (NIV)** – *"Accept him whose faith is weak, without passing judgement on disputable matters. Ones man's faith allows him to eat everything, but another man, whose faith is weak, eats only vegetables. The man who eats everything must not look down on him who does not, and the man who does not eat everything must not condemn the man who does, for God has accepted him."*
>
> **I Corinthians 8:9 (NIV)** – *"Be careful, however, that the exercise of your freedom does not become a stumbling block to the weak."*
>
> **I Corinthians 6:12 (NIV)** – *"Everything is permissible for me – but not everything is beneficial. Everything permissible for me—but I will not be mastered by anything."*

I. Essential Definitions

A. __Ethical Grey Area__: An area that is not specifically addressed in the Bible and is therefore viewed as permissible by some Christians.

B. **Stronger Brother/Sister**: This is a person who __participates__ in an ethical gray area in full assurance of their conscience because of his/her understanding of Christian freedom.

   Note: This does not necessarily mean he/she is more mature in the faith than a weaker brother/sister.

C. **Weaker Brother/Sister**: This is a person who __does not__ participate in an ethical gray area because of the sensitivity of their conscience: his/her participation would be a sin to them.

   Note: This does not necessarily mean he/she is less mature in the faith than a stronger brother/sister.

D. **Stumbling Block**: An action taken by a stronger brother/sister which, though it would ordinarily qualify as a permissible act of freedom, influences a weaker brother/sister to sin against his/her conscience.

How should I make decisions about the following?

Birth Control	Drinking Alcohol	Cussing
Dancing	TV and Movies	Marijuana
Smoking/Snuff	Drugs/Caffeine	Piercings
Working on Sunday	Clothing styles/Modesty	Tattoos

Pre-marital eye contact

II. Principles
A. _Convinced for ourselves_.
   1. We must true to ourselves and not act simply on the opinions of others.
   2. Romans 14:5
   3. Romans 14:22-23
B. _Confident before God_.
   1. If we are confident that we are engaged in will pass our Lord's scrutiny at the judgment day, we should continue; if not, we should refrain.
   2. Romans 14:6-12
C. _Considerate of other believers_.
   1. Romans 14:12-21
   2. To "offend" here does not mean to make angry, but rather to cause another believer to act in such a way.
   3. "Am I my brother's keeper?" –Cain. The spiritual truth is that we are our brother's keeper! (Romans 14:15-20,15:1-6)
D. _Concerned for unbelievers_.
   1. I Corinthians 10:27-33
   2. Paul was burdened enough about unsaved that he restricted himself in doing only what enhanced the gospel in their eyes.

III. Guidelines
A. **Principles of** _Expedience_.
   Will it be spiritually profitable? I Corinthians 6:12
B. **Principle of** _Edification_.
   Will it build me up? I Corinthians 10:23
C. **Principle of** _Excess_.
   Will it slow me down in the race? Hebrews 12:1
D. **Principle of** _Enslavement_.
   Will it bring me into bondage? I Corinthians 6:12
E. **Principle of** _Equivocation_.
   Will it hypocritically cover my sin? I Peter 2:16
F. **Principle of** _Encroachment_.
   Will it violate the Lordship of Christ in my life? Romans 14:1-8
G. **Principle of** _Example_.
   Will it help other Christians by its example? I Corinthians 8:9
H. **Principle of** _Evangelism_.
   Will it lead others to Christ? I Corinthians 10:27-29

I. **Principle of** _Emulation_.
   Would Jesus do it? I John 2:6
J. **Principle of** _Exaltation_.
   Will it glorify God? I Corinthians 10:31
   (These principles were adapted from a sermon by Dr. John MacArthur Jr.)

A Summary on Christian Liberty

L- Liberty not _License_ -Romans 6:14-15

I – Individual Accountability to God – Romans 14:12

B – Biblical truth not Personal _Opinion_ - Psalm 119:10

E – Encourages acceptance not Judgement – Romans 14:3

R – Responsibility to others – Romans 15:1

T – Trust your _Conscience_ - Romans 14:5, 14

Y – Yield your freedom for a Weaker Brother or Sister – Romans 14:15-22

> "Perhaps we should see LIBERTY as a gift that is only <u>gained</u> when it is <u>given,</u> not a <u>right</u> as much as a <u>responsibility</u>, and is best exemplified in <u>peace</u> not <u>pride</u>!"

Chapter 6: Religious Worldviews

Chapter Overview:

Admonition from scripture

Hinduism

Core Beliefs of Hindu Scripture

Hinduism plan of Salvation

Biblical Perspective on Hinduism

Buddhism

Principles & Practices of Buddhism

Sacred Writings

Biblical Perspective on Buddhism

Islam

Theology & Practices of Islam

Islam's Plan of Salvation

Islam since Muhammad

Biblical Perspective on Islam

Comparison: Islam & Christianity

"Whenever there is a decline of Dharma (Righteousness) and a predominance of Adharma (Unrighteousness), O Arjuna, then I manifest myself (become an avatar). I appear from time to time for protecting the good, for transforming the wicked, and for establishing world order. (Dharma)." (Gita, 4.07 -08)

"The best of all paths is the Eightfold Path. The best of all truths are the Four Noble Truths. Non-attachment is the best of all states. The best of all men is the seeing One (the Buddha). This is the only Way. There is none other for the purity of vision. Everything else is…deceit."

The Buddha, Dhamappada, 273-274.

"The Shahada (Arabic, "testimony" or "witness") is the Muslim profession or confession of faith and the first of the Five Pillars in Islam. A translation would be: "There is no god but Allah and Muhammad is the prophet of Allah."

ADMONITION FROM SCRIPTURE

I Peter 3:15 (NIV) *"But in your hearts set apart Christ as Lord. Always be prepared to give an answer to everyone who asks you to give the reason for the hope that you have. But do this with gentleness and kindness."*

John 14:6 (NIV) *"Jesus answered, I am the way and the truth and the life. No one comes to the Father except through me."*

John 17:14-17 (NIV) *"I have given them your word and the world has hated them, for they are not of the world any more than I am of the world. My prayer is not that you take them out of the world but that you protect them from the evil one. They are not of the world, even as I am not of it. Sanctify them by the truth; your word is truth."*

Hinduism

I. **Name, Key Symbol and Number of Followers**
   A. __Dharma__ - righteousness, duty; "Hinduism" a later word applied to people of Indus Valley, now accepted by natives.
   B. Meaning of symbol "OM"
   C. The third largest world religion; roughly around 900 million Hindus worldwide (14% of all religious adherents). About 1 million in U.S.

II. **Brief History**
   A. The Vedic Period (1500 to 300 B.C. – no one really knows)
   B. The __Upanishads__ (800 – 400 B.C.)
   C. Modern Hinduism – Unlike Buddhism, Christianity, and Islam, Hinduism has no single founder and it is also impossible to say exactly what Hinduism is in terms of religious beliefs because there is no one way of understanding "god".

III. **Sacred Writings**
   A. The Vedas – Only Hindu scholars learn and study Vedas now.
   B. The Upanishads
      ➢ Philosophical basis of Hinduism today
      ➢ Central idea –"Atman is Brahman" summed up in "tat tvam asi," lit. "You are that".
   C. The __Epics__
      ➢ Bhagavad- Gita (Between 1000-900 B.C.; Lit. "Song of the Supreme Lord".
      ➢ Mahabharata (Between 540 and 300 B.C. "The Great Bharata" – a family name)
      ➢ The Ramayana (Between 400 and 200 B.C. "The Story of Rama"
      ➢ Main subjects of the Gita
         • Way of salvation explained from philosophy of Upanishads.
         • Indestructibility of the Atman and its oneness with Brahman.

- Duties (dharma) of caste.
- Karma, Samsara and Moksha.
- Supreme value of yoga. (especially karma and bhakti)
- Krishna reveals self as Supreme Being over all gods and people. (Gita 4.06, 10).

IV. Core Beliefs and Hindu Scriptures

Important: This is not a creed or a "doctrinal statement" to determine whether someone is or is not a Hindu. They are not required beliefs, but presently beliefs held by most Hindus.

A. **Brahman** – Most Hindus believe that ultimate Reality is Brahman.
B. ____Atman____ – all humans possess an atman, or eternal and indestructible soul/self and its ultimate destiny and purpose is to be united to Brahman and true Self. Note: Realizing that atman is Brahman is to achieve the highest or perfect knowledge, according to Hinduism.
C. **Maya** – Our perceptions are actually Maya, which means "illusion" or "appearance"; that is, what we experience in our existence, in the natural worlds, is not the really real, kind of like a dream or a mirage – it appears real and we may act as though it is real, but it is an illusion, it is an "illusive power" (Gita 3.29)
D. ____Samsara____ – We are caught up in the illusory world of Maya because of our desires and attachments to the world and its pleasures. As long as the atman does not realize that it is really Brahman, it remains locked in the potentially endless earthly cycle of birth, death and rebirth called Samsara, or literally "a wandering across".
E. **Karma** – the law of karma (cause and effect based on actions/deeds)
   - Keeps people locked in Samsara (Even "good karma)
   - Depending on Karma, may be reincarnated (or return in another physical body) as a human, an animal or even a plant.
   - Good karma still a curse but has some benefits.
   - Temporary heavenly time, then reincarnation in higher caste (thus one step closer to Moksha.)
F. **Moksha** – the hope in Hinduism, the salvation for which Hindus strive, is Moksha. This is "liberation" from Samsara.

Samsara: The endless cycles of death and rebirth.

V. Summarizing Hinduism's Plan of Salvation:

A. **What is salvation?** –*Moksha* – liberation from *Samsara*. Main idea – performing daily duties (dharma) and disciplines in view of union (yoking) with *Brahman.*
B. **What makes salvation necessary?** – Karma and Samsara – We are locked into this never-ending cycle because we have not renounced earthly

31

pleasures and sought union with Brahman. We are ignorant of this true knowledge which keeps us trapped in the illusion.

- C. **What makes salvation possible?** – The explanations found in the Hindu Scriptures, especially the Gita where Krishna tells his followers how to be united to Brahman; the Supreme.
- D. **What makes salvation personal?** – Renunciation of earthly pleasures, fulfilling dharma (caste duty), practicing yoga (focusing mind and body on achieving union with Brahman.)

VI. The Five Worldview Questions Answered from a Hindu Perspective

- A. Origin – There are many stories about creation. The Hindu scriptures provide a variety of ideas about how it occurred. One example is that Brahma is the creator.
- B. Identity – Spiritually, there is no distinction between animals and humans. Animals have souls like humans and are part of the reincarnation process. Each human possess an "atman" (the true self) which goes through the cycles of reincarnation. (Gita, 2:20)
- C. Meaning – The meaning of life has changed over time. The earliest ideas from the Vedas was to sacrifice to the gods and do one's social duty (caste system) by having good karma. In the Upanishads, the emphasis changed to the denial of the trappings if this world to a life of asceticism. To be free from illusion and be reunited with the Brahman (ultimate reality). (Upandishad, 3. 14. 1)
- D. Morality – Living by the moral code of Dharma (the cosmic law of right living). Karma is also associated with morality and one's karma determines one's rebirths.
- E. Destiny – Moksha is the liberation from the reincarnation cycle. This is achieved through performing daily duties (dharma) and uniting with Brahman.

VII. Some Biblical Perspective on Hinduism

Some claim that Hinduism is the "oldest" of the world religions, suggesting it's the beginning of man's religious thought. Christians would have to disagree with this. In Genesis we see the oldest human "religion" and civilization. Biblical narrative conveys that there is one God who created humans in His image and likeness as one male and one female initially; these first humans then fell into corruption. They acquired a sin nature which somehow affected their heart which became "evil only continually." But God promised redemption to these humans and covered their original sins with animal skins, instituting the need for sacrificial atonement to pay for sin. When humanity became utterly corrupt, God destroyed the world through a worldwide, catastrophic flood, after which Noah's family became the basis of all current civilizations, including that which settled in the Indus Valley. In Genesis Chapter 10 we see how from Noah and his sons descended all the nations (10:32). In chapter 11 we learn how the world was populated from the incident at Babel. Languages changed and people dispersed.

Once these early ancestors spread out, they took ideas of the true religion—the true story of humankind regarding creation, the fall, the need for sacrificial atonement for sins, and the flood to many other parts of the world. They eventually, due to their sin nature, distorted these ideas into polytheism - assigning separate gods to the parts of creation (which early Hinduism did)—but still retained ideas consistent with a biblical theology; like an original creation, a worldwide flood, moral obligations, etc. Paul, in fact, states clearly that humanity has always known the truth about God, but, due to their sinfulness, suppressed that truth, and "exchanged the truth of God for a lie, and worshipped and served the creature more than the Creator (Romans 1:19-25)." The multiple depictions of Hindu gods as animals, humans and mixtures of both, is part of the distortion when they "changed the glory of the incorruptible God into images of corruptible man, and birds and four-footed beasts and creeping things (Romans 1:23).

We should not be surprised that we find similarities in religions like Hinduism, because God created the human heart (Psalm 33:15) and placed eternity (Ecclesiastes 3:11) and a sense of morality (Romans 2:14-15) in it. Religions, thus, always convey morality (and very similar ones at that) and a sense of eternal life no matter where they are in the world; what we might call a sense of always (a yearning for immortality) and a sense of ought (an inescapable sense of moral law).

Hinduism and Christianity Contrasted

Topic	Hinduism	Christianity
God	Impersonal	Personal
Humanity	Continuous in the sense of being extended from the being of God.	Discontinuous in the sense of being separate from the Being of God; continuous in the sense of being made in God's image.
Humanity's Problem	Ignorance	Moral rebellion
The Solution	Liberation from illusion	Forgiveness of sin and reconciliation with the personal Holy God.
The Means	Detachment from desire and awareness of unity with the divine through self-effort.	Repentance from sin and trusting in the completed and substitutionary work of Jesus Christ.
The Outcome	Merge into the Oneness; the individual disappears.	Eternal fellowship with God; the person is fulfilled in a loving relationship with God.

Buddhism

I. Name, Key Symbol and Number of Followers
   A. Buddha and Buddhism
   B. The Wheel of Dharma (or Dhamma) or Dharma/Dhamma Wheel.
   C. Fourth largest world religion with about 376 million followers worldwide (about 6% of all religious believers are Buddhist) and 1.5 million Buddhists in the U.S.

II. Brief History
   A. A Renegade __Hindu__.
- Buddhism was founded by Siddhartha Gautama during the sixth century B.C His life (563-483 B.C) coincided with the time when the people of Judah were exiled in Babylon.
- Four Signs — *Elderly person – sick person – corpse – poor monk*
- The Great Renunciation

   B. Discovering the __Middle Path__.
- Life offers only *dukkha* – which means suffering, misery, frustration, unsatisfied desires, disease and death.
- Six years of asceticism – nearly starved himself to death and concluded that such self-denial was too extreme and "profitless"
- The Middle Path/ *Dhamma* – Gautama's unique contribution to religious thought: That balanced "path" between the "two extremes" of "a life given to pleasures and lusts" and "a life given to mortifications" (harsh self –denial of not just bodily wants but bodily needs), both of which he had come to see as "profitless."

III. Central Principles and Practices of Buddhism

<u>The Four Noble Truths</u>

   A. **The First Noble Truth** (The certainty of suffering): Life consists of __suffering__ (dukkha). This concept of suffering includes the experience of pain, misery, sorrow, and un-fulfillment.

   B. **The Second Noble Truth** (The source/cause of suffering): Everything is impermanent and __tanah__ (the doctrine of *anicca*). We suffer because we desire those things that are impermanent.

   C. **The Third Noble Truth** (The cessation/cure of suffering): the way to liberate oneself from suffering is by eliminating __desire (Tanah)__. We must stop craving that which is temporary.

   D. **The Fourth Noble Truth** (The path to the cessation of suffering): Desire can be eliminated by following the Eightfold Path, which consists of eight points that can be categorized according to three major sections:

The Practice of Buddhism (The Noble Eightfold Path)

Wisdom (*Panna*)
1. Right **Views (understanding)**
2. Right **Intent (Thoughts)**

Ethical Conduct (*Sila*)
3. Right **Speech**
4. Right **Action**
5. Right **Livelihood**

Mental Discipline (*Smadhi*)
6. Right **Effort**
7. Right **Concentration (Awareness)**
8. Right **Mindfulness (meditation)**

> These eight points are not steps to be taken in sequential order, but are attitudes and actions to be developed simultaneously. The first two points, moreover, serve as the foundation from which the other points flow.

Further Principles of Buddhism

Nirvana in *Buddhism* (The Goal)

- Not heaven or paradise, not a place that one goes when they die
- A passionless state where one feels neither love nor hate
- Literal meaning of Nirvana **Cessation**.

IV. Sacred Writings

A. *Tipitaka* - the "Three Baskets" – 3 main sections of Buddhist scriptures; passed on orally by monks and nuns until committed to writing some 400 years after Buddha's death. (Like builders passing building materials in baskets.)
B. *Sutta –Pitaka* – **Gautama's sermons and dialogues, called Sutta**
   - The *Dhamapadda* – Most popular part of *Sutta*; collection of Gautama's core ideas in 432 maxims.
   - The *Jatakas* – stories illustrating Buddha's teachings recalling his past lives (as animals) before coming to the one in which he would finally experience enlightenment and escape samsara.
C. *Vinaya Pitaka* – Rules for Monks and Nuns

D. *Abhidhamma Pitaka* – Philosophical teachings explaining the Buddhist worldview underlying the practicalities of the Eight-fold path.

V. Two Major Division/Schools of Buddhism
A. <u>Theravada (Hinayana)</u> Buddhism –Traditional, Conservative, or Orthodox
B. <u>Mahayana</u> Buddhism –Liberal sect whose name literally means, "great vehicle"

VI. Summarizing Buddhism's Plan of Salvation
A. *What is salvation?* – Liberation from suffering and what causes it, achieving Nirvana.
B. *What makes salvation necessary?* –potentially endless cycles of rebirth and death (Samsara)
C. *What makes salvation possible?* – The Buddha's personal discovery, example and teachings.
D. *What makes salvation personal?* – Believing the Four Noble Truths and practicing the Noble Eightfold Path.

VII. The Five Worldview Questions Answered from a Buddhist Perspective
A. Origin – According to Buddha, everything is Samsara, a part of the endless cycle of birth, death and rebirth. He did not address this issue since it had no meaning or value.
B. Identity – Animals and humans are both sentient (conscious) beings. Humans can be reborn as animals and animals can be reborn as humans.
C. Meaning – To detach oneself from the cravings of this world, which produces Dukkha (suffering). This is achieved through following the Four Noble truth about suffering and following the Noble Eightfold Path.
D. Morality – This is Sila and is described as virtue, or one part of the Eightfold Path (Right Conduct). However, right and wrong do not exist but one should follow, that which is personally beneficial.
E. Destiny – Humans have an equal chance to reach Nirvana by eliminating desire. Nirvana is not a place but a cessation of existence or passionless state.

VIII. Some Biblical Perspective on Buddhism

Some suggest that Jesus and Buddha really taught essentially the same things, that their doctrines are compatible. This is both true and not true. From an ethical perspective, Buddhism has a lot of merit in that Gautama's and Jesus' moral doctrines are similar. This, we could attribute to the moral law of God "written on the heart" (Romans 2:14-15) and should not find it surprising that all religions, not just Buddhism, teach very similar moral principles. Because of this, much of the ethical teaching and

stories of Gautama can be illuminating and illustrative to Jesus' followers.
But here is where the comparison ends. Theologically, Jesus and Gautama are at two opposite poles. Jesus was a monotheist and believed in and taught that God was personal and could be related to as intimately as a "Father" who created man and woman in his image and sustains His creation in a very active way. Jesus taught and modeled prayer to the Father. His use of the intimate term "Abba" is quite significant in this regard. (Mk 14:36) He teaches his followers to pray "Our Father Who is in Heaven (Matthew 6:9) this intimacy with God as a personal, heavenly Father is also taught by Paul (Romans 8:15, Galatians 4:6).

Jesus also believed the source of our sorrows came from within, due to an indwelling sin nature and core corruption, not merely desire or craving (Mark 7:21-22). So, a huge and significant contrast is that Jesus taught that we needed to be forgiven of sin by our Heavenly Father (Matthew 6:12). He also taught about the Kingdom of Heaven as though it were a place in the afterlife that one could aspire to and dwell in, as well as a present reality (Matthew 5:20), and thus escape the condemnation of a literal hell. Jesus also spoke of death and resurrection and a final judgment (John 5:29), never reincarnation.

Probably the greatest significance is the contrast in how Jesus and Gautama thought of themselves and their importance for humanity. Gautama told his followers not to remember him, *per se,* but his teachings as the most important thing. In fact, contrary to popular opinion, Gautama was quite adamant that his teachings were superior to all others. He taught, "The best of ways is the eightfold; the best of truths is the four words (noble truths); the best of virtues is passionlessness, *this is the way, there is no other* that leads to the purifying of intelligence. Go on this way! Everything else is . . . deceit. (*Dhamapadda* 20:273-4). Jesus, on the other hand did not point to his teachings as "the way" but rather to Himself as *the* way, *the* truth and *the* life." (John 14:6) His disciples/apostles followed suit when they pronounced "neither is there
salvation in any other, for there is no other name under heaven given among men by which we must be saved" (Acts 4:12)

This cannot be overemphasized. While Jesus was humble and considered one wise who built his life on His teachings (Matthew 7:24-27), He unequivocally conveyed that getting his identity right was critical to our eternal well-being. "Who do you say that I am?" (Matthew 16:15), "If you do not believe that I am He, you will die in your sins." (John 8:24) "He who does not believe the Son does not have life . . . but God's wrath abides on him." (John 3:36) and "No one comes to the Father except through me." (John 14:6). Jesus made it clear that remembering Him (Luke 22:19) and believing in Him alone for salvation was critical to being His follower and entering the kingdom of Heaven to live eternally with God; there was no other way. So while Gautama taught high moral principles, and claimed to point the way, leaving us some great quotes and illustrations, Jesus Christ was far more than a great moral teacher, and claimed to *be* the way.

Buddhism and Christianity Contrasted

Topic	Theravada Buddhism	Mahayana Buddhism	Christianity
God	Nirvana, an abstract Void.	Nirvana, an abstract Void, but also an undifferentiated Buddha essence.	A personal God who is self-existent and changeless.
Humanity	An impermanent collection of aggregates.	An impermanent collection of aggregates. For some, personal existence continues for a while in the Pure Land.	Made in God's image. Personal existence has value. We continue to exist as persons after death.
Humanity's Problem	We suffer because we desire that which is temporary, and we continue in the illusion of the existence of the self.	Same as Theravada.	We suffer because of the consequences of our sin. But we also suffer because, being made in God's image, we are fulfilled only when we are in a relationship with our Creator God. But we have rebelled against God, and are thus alienated from Him.
The Solution	To cease all desire and to realize the nonexistence of the self, thus finding permanence.	To become aware of the Buddha nature within.	To be forgiven by and reconciled with God. We fine permanence in the immutability of God.
The Means	Self-reliance. We must follow the Middle Path, and accrue karmic merit.	Self-reliance. The means vary from following the Eightfold Path, to emptying the mind, to accruing merit by performing rituals, to realizing the Buddha-nature within, to depending on the merits of bodhisattva.	Reliance on God. We must repent of our sins and trust in the saving work of Jesus Christ.
The Outcome	To enter nirvana where the ego is extinguished.	The outcome varies from that of returning as a bodhisattva in order to guide others, to living in a Pure Land from which one can enter Nirvana, to entering nirvana.	Our existence as individuals survives death, and we are fulfilled as we are in eternal fellowship with a loving and personal God.

Islam

I. Name, Key Symbol and Number of Followers
A. Islam, Muslim – The word Islam means "_Submission_" and refers to the lifestyle of the true "Muslim" (submitter) in submission to the one God's will.
B. The crescent moon and star – (origin unknown but generally associated with Islam)
C. Second largest world religion, about 1.5 billion Muslims worldwide (nearly 21% of all religious believers.) There are approximately 1.6 million Muslims in the U.S.

II. Brief History
A. An orphan in _Mecca_
   1. Raised by paternal uncle – Muhammad (whose name means "highly praised") was born in 570 A.D. in Mecca. His father died before he was born, and his mother died when he was six. For two years after that he was raised by his grandfather until he, too, died and his paternal uncle, Abu Talib, raised him in the city of Mecca.

   2. Muhammad's marriage – At age 25 he married an older woman named Khadija, a wealthy caravan owner whose caravan he tended.

   3. Muhammad's spiritual leanings – Muhammad often retired to a cave in the surrounding mountains to meditate and pursue his spiritual interests. He was troubled by the religious practices of the Meccans, especially because of the idolatry and immorality.

B. The Reading/Recitation
   1. At age 40 Muhammad, in the month of Ramadan in 610 A.D., while in a cave on Hira, was visited by an angel *Jibril* (Gabriel), holding a scroll. Throughout the rest of his life Muhammad received further revelations. Believing these were, indeed, from God, Muhammed ensured that others wrote down the words he would utter. He often went into trances before uttering the words of the *Qur'an*.
   2. Allah is one. The chief message at the heart of the *Qur'an's* theology was that God is one and has no partners or equals and to believe that he does is the ultimate blasphemy.

C. The Conflict
Although Muhammad's influence was minor at first, more and more people listened and followed his teachings. As his following became larger, more visible and outspoken, the natives of Mecca began to see Muhammad, his teaching and his growing community/brotherhood (*umma*) as a threat and began persecuting them. In the year 622 A.D. Muhammad and his followers left Mecca and went about 280 miles north to *Yathrib* (later called Medina; "the city" of the Prophet), and there established Islam as a theocracy. There, the people were far more receptive and eager for Muhammad's message. This exodus from Mecca is called the *Hijrah* or "emigration" and marks the beginning of the Islamic calendar.

D. The Importance of Mecca
Despite his reception and success in Medina, Muhammad still wanted Mecca. The main reason for this was that the Kaaba was in Mecca, the location where it is believed,

Abraham offered Ishmael (not Isaac as the Bible states) to Allah in obedience, symbolizing the ultimate in submission (*Islam*) to God.

III. The Qur'an
   A. Meaning and Arrangement "<u>Recitation</u>" – The word Qur'an literally means "recitation" and refers to its being revealed to Muhammad and recited by him to be written down and read for all true followers of Allah.

   B. 114 surahs (chapters)

IV. Core Theology and Practices of Islam

Question: Do Muslims and Christians worship the same God? "Both Christians and Muslims share belief in sovereign Deity who is one, heavenly, spiritual, the creator of heaven and earth and the judge of all mankind. Christians call Him "***God***" and Muslims call Him "***Allah***". One may thus presume that the attributes of God and Allah are the same. A careful examination of the matter, however, will prove that it is not exactly so." – Abdullah Al Araby, *God of Christianity vs. Allah of Islam*, http://www.islamreview.com/articles/godvsallah.shtml July 2012

Muhammad with the Qur'an

   A. **The Five Core Beliefs**
      1. The oneness/unity of Allah
      2. The Prophets/Messengers of Islam with primacy of Muhammad
      3. The Scriptures with primacy on the Qur'an
      4. Angelic Activity
      5. The Day of Resurrection and Final Judgement

   B. **The Five Pillars of Islam**
      1. The Confession of Faith (*Shahada*)
      2. The Contact Prayers (*Salat*)
      3. Alms or Poor Tax (*Zakat*)
      4. Fasting during Ramadan
      5. The Pilgrimage to Mecca (*Hajj*)

V. Summarizing Islam's Plan of Salvation
   A. *What is salvation?* – Entering Paradise on Judgment Day and escaping Hell.
   B. *What makes salvation necessary?* – Humanity's forgetfulness/ignorance of Allah's Oneness and the Qur'an; and sure, damnation if Alah is not remembered and obeyed.
   C. *What makes salvation possible?* – Revelation of the Qur'an to Muhammad; it is called, among other things a "mercy" and a "guide" to humanity to find submission, the true religion.

D. *What makes salvation personal?* – Submission to Allah as demonstrated by strict adherence to the Five Pillars.

VI. The Five Worldview Questions Answered from an Islamic Perspective
A. Origin – Allah was active in creating the world (Qur'an 21:31-33), but many Muslims accept the theory of evolution as well.
B. Identity – All people are born Muslims, but Islam teaches all to willfully submit to Allah. Humans were not created in Allah's image. Humans can use and eat animals but not with cruelty. Humans alone have volition but both can praise Allah.
C. Meaning or purpose – The word "Islam" means submission. Humanity's purpose is to submit to Allah by following the Qur'an and teachings in the Hadith
D. Morality – One is moral when one believes in Allah, follows the Five Pillars, as well as the teachings of the Qur'an and Hadith.
E. Destiny – Humans will be sent to Paradise or Hell based upon their works and the will of Allah.

VI. Islam since Muhammad
A. Death of Muhammad and Division of Muslims
  1. The Sunnis- 80 -90% Worldwide
  2. The Shiites – 10-20% Worldwide

The two major sects of Islam, Sunni and Shiite, were divided originally over a dispute as to who should serve as the first caliph, or successor, to Muhammad, who had failed to appoint one before his death. The Sunni Muslims insisted that Muhammad's successor should be elected. The Shiite (or Shia'h) Muslims thought he should come through Muhammad's bloodline, which would have meant Ali, Muhammad's cousin and son-in-law, would be his successor.

B. Islam and Jihad – Arabic for "struggle"
  1. Primary Meaning- Struggling with one's self and the world to live out one's faith. (Similar to idea of "spiritual warfare" in Christianity)
  2. "Holy War" – Struggling (fighting) against the enemies of Allah. This is to a translation of Jihad, but an interpretation.

VII. *Some Biblical Perspective on Islam*

Of the three non-Christian religious we have examined, Islam is closest to Christianity. In fact, as we have mentioned, the Qur'an even speaks very highly of Jesus, but while this is the case, it does not honor Jesus as God, which the Bible says, clearly, we are to do (John 5:23). Let's briefly examine this Jesus question, and demonstrate how Islam and Christianity are not teaching the same thing at all when it comes to the true worship of God and why this even matters. In the Qur'an, surah 3:42-60, we find a very lengthy teaching about Jesus, much of which is consistent with the Gospels. His birth was preannounced to Mary, he was born of a virgin, He will be obeyed and teach obedience to the disciples (meaning they were Muslims, of course), he performed miracles like healing the lepers, the blind and raising the dead (a claim Muhammad could not make). Jesus, unlike any other messenger of Allah, was said to be "supported/strengthened… with the Holy Spirit." (???) Jesus alone, was given "the Gospel" (5:46, 57:27). Jesus is regularly identified in the Qur'an as "Messiah" which no other prophet, including Muhammad, is designated.

Despite these amazingly positive and even biblical things said about Jesus, the Qur'an denies two very central biblical teachings which happen to undermine the essence of Christianity. According to surah 4:157-158 Jesus was not crucified, but in a slight of hand, Allah made it "appear" that the Jews had slain Jesus. Instead, Allah "took him up" to himself (although we don't know exactly what this means). Messiah's/Christ's literal death is central to the Bible (Isaiah 53 and I Corinthians) and the heart of the gospel. Christianity is nothing without the crucifixion of Christ, and his unique resurrection "from the dead".

More troubling, however, is the *Qur'an's* blatant denial of Jesus' deity. Of course, this grows out of the doctrine of Allah's oneness, making it impossible that he could have equal "partners" in heaven. A related idea attacked by this is Jesus' being the "son" of God.

According to the *Qur'an*, God cannot have a son (2:116, 4:171, 6:101) and that there is "no warrant" (10:68), for such a claim. To suggest this is "a disastrous thing" with potentially devastating cosmic effects (19:88-93). In fact, at some points Jesus, the Messiah, son of Mary (as the *Qur'an* frequently refers to him), is the very one who denies his own sonship and deity, pronouncing severe judgment on any who would suggest otherwise (5:72-3). It follows from this that Jesus was "no other than a messenger," indistinct from all previous messengers (2:136, 4:171), and nothing other than a human, just like Adam (3:59), which, of course, annuls any idea of Jesus' pre-existence. Jesus accepted his status as a mere "slave" of Allah (19:30, 33, 43:59; like we all should), and even predicts the coming of Muhammad, whose name would be "even more praised" (61:6) than his.

To answer this challenge, we need to compare/contrast the biblical view of Jesus, and what He claimed about himself, to the Qur'an's depiction of Jesus. For sake of time, we will limit this analysis to the Gospel of John in which Jesus' deity is unequivocally proclaimed with a purpose to guide us into believing that He is the Christ, the son of God, and that believing we might have life in His name (John 20:31).

In John's "prologue," Jesus is clearly identified as the pre-existing, eternal, Word, equivalent with God (1:1-2). The Word was the agent of creation of all things, including the world (1:3, 10 see also Colossians 1:16-17 and Hebrews 1:2). The eternal Word which dwelt with God and was God and which created all things was "made flesh and dwelt among us" and was the "son" who made the Father known to the world during his earthly sojourn (1:18, see also Colossians 1:19, 2:9 and Hebrews 1:3). This remarkable passage has already established Jesus' pre-existence, His equality with God, His being the creator of all things, and His sonship, making known "the Father" to the world; all things denied by the Qur'an. The rest of John's gospel clearly establishes Jesus' sonship and deity, and this is the critical issue for humans to believe so that they might be forgiven of their sins and have eternal life.

The self-understanding of Jesus we find in the Bible is clearly poles apart from that which we see in the *Qur'an*. As we have seen, in the gospel of John alone Jesus explicitly claims to be the "Son of God" (which is equivalent to a claim to deity), and to have pre- existed with the "Father" "in heaven" prior to His appearance on earth. He claims to have "come from heaven" and not to have originated in the world like all humans, He asserts his sinlessness, and how this qualifies His doctrine as authoritative and certifies his oneness with God. He also predicts his literal death and its purpose, and explains that he, as God alone, has the power to forgive sins. Jesus Christ and His message about Himself as the Son of God and the one in whom we must place our saving faith is all that matters.

Suggested Reading

Anyabwile, Thabiti. "The Gospel for Muslims: An Encouragement to Share Christ with Confidence." Chicago: Moody, 2010.

Braswell, George. Islam: Prophet, Peoples, Politics, and Power. Nashville: Broadman and Holman, 1996.

Geisler, Norman L., and Abdul Saleeb. *Answering Islam: The Crescent in Light of the Cross.* Grand Rapids, MI: Baker, 1993.

Komoszewski, J. Ed., M. James Sawyer, and Daniel B. Wallce. *Reinventing Jesus: How Contemporary Skeptics Miss the Real Jesus and Mislead Popular Culture.* Grand Rapids, MI: Kregel, 2006.

Saleeb. "Islam." In *To Everyone an Answer: A Case for the Christian Worldview : Essays in Honor of Norman L. Geisler*. Edited by Norman L. Geisler, Francis Beckwith, William Lane Craig, and James Porter Moreland. Downers Grove, Ill: InterVarsity Press, 2004.

Swartley, Keith. *Encountering the World of Islam*. Waynesboro, GA: Authentic, 2005.

Salvation Comparison Chart

	Islam	Buddhism	Hinduism	Christianity
What is salvation?	Being **rewarded** on Judgement Day with entrance into Paradise if one's righteous deeds are determined to outweigh their sinful deeds.	Achievement of **Nirvana** – **"Cessation"** of desire and the suffering that comes from desire, including the cycles of death and rebirth.	Achievement of **Moksha** – **"Liberation"** from the painful cycle of death and rebirth. **Realization** of one's unity with the Ultimate Reality (Brahman)	Being **rescued** from sin's eternal consequences, temporal control and actual condition. **Receiving** eternal life as a **gift** of grace.
What makes salvation necessary?	Humans are ignorant of their true nature as a Muslim (submitter) and destined for Hell's fire until they submit to Allah's will.	Humans are **enslaved** by *karma* to *samsara* because of their **desire** for the impermanent things of this world, and the experience endless **suffering** due to this.	Humans, because of *karma*, are trapped in the cycle of death and rebirth (*samsara*) because of their **ignorance** of Ultimate Reality, and attachment to worldly illusion (*maya*).	Humans are **sinful** and are **separated** from and **subject** to the **eternal wrath** of a Holy and Righteous God.
What makes salvation possible?	The **Qur'an** which teaches humans of their true identity as Muslims who must willingly submit to the will of Allah…	The enlightenment, **example and teachings of Siddhartha Guatama** who became the Buddha through overcoming his desire.	The **knowledge** found in the Hindu Scriptures about escaping Karma and samsara and achieving moksha and one's ultimate unity with Brahman.	**Divine initiative**: God through **love** and **grace** reveals the **gospel** and provides to rescue humans from sin through the substitutionary **death and resurrection of Jesus Christ.**
What makes salvation personal?	*Human Effort*: **Confessing** in the **Shahada**; believing the **Articles of Faith** and practicing the **Five Pillars of Islam**.	*Human Effort*: Accepting the **Four Noble Truths** and following the **Noble Eightfold Path**. Taking refuge in Buddha, *Dhamma* (his teachings) and *Sangha* (community of fellow Buddhists)	*Human Effort*: **Becoming a yogi** (one who practices yoga, a discipline by which can realize oneness with Ultimate Reality); **Living faithfully** to one's given station in life (*caste* and *dharma*).	*Repentance* and *Faith*: Owning up to ad turning from one's sin and turning to the Savior, Jesus Christ, alone for salvation and submitting to him as Lord.

Chapter 7:
Tolerance

Chapter Overview:

Admonition from Scripture

Tolerance Defined

Two Kinds of Tolerance

The New Tolerance

The Biblical View

The Cost of Tolerance

Tolerance and the Christian

"Notice that one can't tolerate someone unless he disagrees with him. We don't "tolerate" people who share our views. They're on our side. There's nothing to put up with. Tolerance is reserved for those we think are wrong.

This essential element of tolerance – disagreement—has been completely lost in the modern distortion of the concept. Nowadays, if you think someone is wrong, you're called intolerant.

This presents us with a very curious problem judging someone wrong makes one intolerant, yet one must first think another is wrong in order to be tolerant. It's a "Catc -22." According to this approach, true tolerance is impossible."

— Greg Koukl www.str.org

"With the current emphasis on multiculturalism and appreciation for the cultural diversity that exists in much of the world, and the importance of a culture's values in it self-definition, it should not surprise us that there is a movement toward accepting all cultures' values as equally valid, which is the definition of cultural relativism."

— Scott B. Rae, Moral Choices: An Introduction to Ethics

ADMONITION FROM SCRIPTURE

Romans 12:18 (NIV) *"If it is possible, as far as it depends on you, live at peace with everyone."*
I Peter 3:15 (NIV) *"But in your hearts set apart Christ as Lord. Always be prepared to give an answer to everyone who asks you to give the reason for the hope that you have. But do this with gentleness and respect."*
Romans 1:15-16 (NIV) *"That is why I am so eager to preach the gospel also to you who are at Rome. I am not ashamed of the gospel, because it is the power of God for the salvation of everyone who believes: first for the Jew, then for the Gentile."*
Ephesians 4:14-15 (KJV) *"That we [henceforth] be no more children, tossed to and fro, and carried about with every wind of doctrine, by the sleight of men, [and] cunning craftiness, whereby they lie in wait to deceive; (15) But speaking in the truth in love, may grow up into him in all things, which is the head, [even] Christ."*
2 Timothy 2:24-26 (NLT) *"The Lord's servants must not quarrel but must be kind to everyone. They must be able to teach effectively and be patient with difficult people. They should gently teach those who oppose the truth. Perhaps God will change those people's hearts, and they will believe the truth. Then they will come to their senses and escape from the Devil's trap. For they have been held captive by him to do whatever he wants."*

I. **Tolerance Defined:**
   Webster's defined tolerate as "to recognize and respect [other's beliefs, practices, etc.] without sharing them," and "to bear or put up with [someone or something not especially liked].

> Note: To tolerate implies that we disagree. We don't "tolerate" people or ideas that share our views because there is nothing to "put up with".

II. **Two kinds of Tolerance:**

   A. **Traditional Tolerance**

   1. Tolerance should be viewed in reference to how we __respond__ to people we disagree with, not how we respond to the _____ we think are false. Even those with whom you disagree and those who are different from you.

   2. Listening to and learning from other __perspectives__, cultures, and backgrounds.

   3. Living peaceably alongside others, in spite of differences.

4. Accepting other people, regardless of their ___race___, ___creed___, nationality, or sex.

5. Traditional tolerance ___values___, ___respects___, and ___accepts___ the individual without the necessarily approving of or participating in his/her beliefs or behavior.

B. **The New Tolerance**

To be truly tolerant, you must agree that another person's position is just valid as your own. You must give your ___approval___, your endorsement, your sincere ___support___ to their ___beliefs___ and ___behaviors___.

1. The new tolerance is vastly different from traditional tolerance.
   ➤ It is based on the belief that "truth is relative to the community in which a person participates. And since there are many human communities, there are necessarily many different truths."
   ➤ "Since truth is described by language, and all language is created by humans, all truth is created by humans."
   ➤ If all truth is created by humans, and all humans are "created equal," then all truth is equal.

2. In contrast to traditional tolerance, which asserts that everyone has an equal right to believe or say what he thinks is right, the new tolerance says that what every individual believes or says is ___equally true___, and ___valid___.

III. The Biblical View

The Bible makes it clear that all values, beliefs, lifestyles, and truth claims are not equally valid.

A. It teaches that the God of the Bible is the true God (Jeremiah 10:10)
B. All of His words are true (Psalm 119:160)
C. If something is not right in God's sight, it is wrong (Deut. 6:18)

IV. The Cost of Tolerance

Proponents of the new tolerance have no problem being intolerant to Christians, Christianity, and the Christian morality because those things present problems for the new tolerance in four basic areas.

A. _Biblical Truth_
B. _Jesus and the Cross_
C. _Sin_
D. _The Mission of the Church_

V. Tolerance and the Christian

The Bible makes it clear how Christians are to act toward each other and toward those outside of the faith.

A. Romans 12:16 *"Be of the same mind toward one another. Do not set your mind on high things but associate with the humble. Do not be wise in your own opinion."*
B. Romans 12:18 *"If it is possible, as much as depends on you, live peaceably with all men."*
C. Ephesians 4:1-2 *"I, therefore, the prisoner of the Lord, beseech you to walk worthy of the calling with which you were called, 2 with all lowliness and gentleness, with longsuffering, bearing with one another in love,"*
D. Ephesians 4:32 *"And be kind to one another, tenderhearted, forgiving one another, even as God in Christ forgave you."*
E. Colossians 3:13 *"bearing with one another, and forgiving one another, if anyone has a complaint against another; even as Christ forgave you, so you also must do."*
F. Galatians 6:10 *"Therefore, as we have opportunity, let us do good to all especially to those who are of the household faith."* (All verses in NKJV)

In all this we must still stand up for and speak the TRUTH in love

Chapter 8:
Abortion

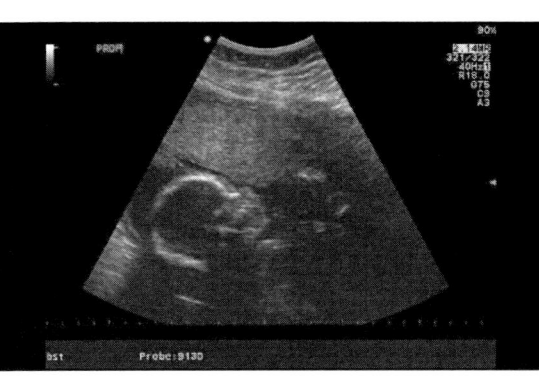

Chapter Overview:

Admonition from Scripture

Abortion Defined

Legal History

Key Legal Cases

Types of Abortions

Arguments

A Helping Strategy

Abortion and Guilt

Readings for Healing

"I feel the greatest destroyer of peace today is 'Abortion', because it is a war against the child... A direct killing of the innocent child, 'Murder' by the mother herself... And if we can accept that a mother can kill even her own child, how can we tell other people not to kill one another? How do we persuade a woman not to have an abortion? As always, we must persuade her with love... And we remind ourselves that love means to be willing to give until it hurts..."

Mother Teresa - *Excepts from her 1979 Nobel Peace Prize speech*

"I think we have deluded ourselves into believing that people don't know that abortion is killing. So, any pretense that abortion is not killing is a signal of our ambivalence, a signal that we cannot say yes, it kills a fetus."

Faye Wattleton, Former President of Planned Parenthood - "Speaking Frankly," Ms., May / June 1997, Volume VII, Number 6, 67.

"Abortion is a real moral issue with real lives at stake, and no amount of leftist badgering could back conservative Americans off their attempts to protect the unborn."

Shapiro, Ben (2018). *And We All Fall Down.* Creators Publishing.

ADMONITION FROM SCRIPTURE

Psalm 139:13-14 (NKJV) *"For you formed my inward parts; you covered me in my mother's womb. I will praise You, for I am fearfully and wonderfully made: Marvelous are Your works, and that my soul knows very well."*
Exodus 20:13 (NIV) *"You shall not murder",*
Jeremiah 1:5 (NIV) *"Before I formed you in the womb I knew [a] you, before you were born I set you apart; I appointed you as a prophet to the nations."*

Abortion defined from a Biblical/ Christian Worldview:

The deliberate termination of a human being from the moment of conception until just prior to birth.

Note: Abortion is often made to sound innocuous. However, in an abortion, not only is the pregnancy or the product of conception terminated, so is a human being. Medical dictionaries define abortion only after implantation. This creates confusion among women considering emergency birth control. www.womenshealth.gov.

I. Abortion: Legal History in the United States.
  A. Prior to Roe V. Wade, most states made abortion a crime except for the saving the mother.
  B. Legal cases that led to Roe v. Wade

   1. _Griswold_ v. _Conneticut_ -Decided June 7, 1965
      Griswold was director of planned parenthood. Married couple didn't know contraception. He told them and got arrested. Parents had a right to privacy in sexual relations

   2. _Eisenstadt_ v. _Baird_ - Decided March 22, 1972
      Baird professor at Boston College. Talked about contraception pills at a (vagina) in a box, shows class, got arrested, privacy between single. All people have privacy due to the two court case

  C. Roe v. Wade – Jan. 22, 1973
   1. Situation: Jane Roe (Norma McCorvey) – *Single woman with unwanted pregnancy challenged present abortion*
   2. Main Ruling: Lifted bans on abortion in all 50 states A woman's "right to privacy" extends to her liberty to terminate an unwanted pregnancy.

3. What the Supreme Court declared:
    ➢ "The Constitution does not define 'person'…" "person" has "application only postnatally"
    ➢ "The word 'person' as used in the Fourteenth Amendment, does not include the unborn."

The unborn are essentially non-persons and do not fall under the protection of the Fourteenth Amendment.

<u>Amendment XIV Section 1 to the U.S. Constitution:</u> All persons born or naturalized in the Unites States, and subject to the jurisdiction thereof, are citizens of the United States… nor shall any State deprive any person of life, liberty, or property, without due process of law; nor deny to any person within its jurisdiction the equal protection of the laws.

II. Key Legal Cases

A. __Roe__ v __Wade__ – Jan. 22, 1973

Main Ruling – Lifted bans on abortion in all 50 states. A woman's "right to privacy" extends to her liberty to terminate an unwanted pregnancy. Also: the unborn are not "persons" and thus ineligible for constitutional protection.

B. __Doe__ v. __Bolton__ – Jan. 22, 1973

Main Ruling – It expanded the definition of the "health" of the mother to include familial, financial and psychological issues etc. as determined by her physician.

C. __Webster__ v. __Reproductive health services__ –1989

Main Ruling – Public money and/or facilities cannot be used to perform abortions.

D. __Planned Parenthood__ v. __Casey__ –1992

Main Ruling – Discarded 3 trimesters of Roe and focused on the "viability" of the fetus as the determining point where a state's interest in unborn life begins.

E. __Partial__ – 2003

WASHINGTON, D.C – President Bush signed the Partial- Birth Abortion Ban Act (S.3) into law on November 3, 2003, the bill represents the first direct national restriction on any method of abortion since the Supreme Court legalized abortion on demand in 1973.

F. _Gonzales vs Carhart_ - 2007

Main Ruling: Upheld as constitutional the federal Partial-Birth Abortion Ban Act of 2003.

G. Supreme Court Ruling - 2022

Main Ruling: Thomas E. Dobbs, State Health Officer for the Mississippi Department of Health banned abortion after 15 weeks. This banned abortion pre-viability. The Jackson Women's Health Organization sued. It went to the U.S. Supreme Court.
Supreme Court ruling on June 24, 2022

- In a 6-3 vote, it affirmed Mississippi's right to regulate abortion. It also stated that the constitution does not confer a right to an abortion. States can decide through their legislation abortion laws.

- In a 5-4 vote, the Supreme Court overturned Roe v. Wade and Planned Parenthood v Casey – Justice John Roberts did not vote to overturn Roe.

III. Types of Abortion

A. _Birth Control Methods_

1. IUD's – Originally, all IUDs stopped implantation. Today, cooper IUDs kill sperm and inhibit fertilization. However, as a secondary measure, if fertilization does occur, it stops the implantation of that fertilized egg.

2. Plan B or the Morning After Pill (Up to 54% of abortions today are medication abortions. It is a one-step pill that contains the hormone levonorgestrel — a progestin — which can prevent ovulation, block fertilization, or keep a fertilized egg from implanting in the uterus.
 * Used up to 72 hours after unprotected sex.
 * Each pill contains levonorgestrel, a synthetic version of the hormone progestin.
 * Plan B One-Step works like other birth control pills to prevent pregnancy. If fertilization does occur, Plan B One-Step may prevent a fertilized egg from attaching to the womb. If a fertilized egg is implanted prior to taking Plan B One-Step, the drug will not work and pregnancy proceeds normally.

3. Birth control pill (Rare)
 a. Stage 1- Prevent ovulation
 b. Stage 2 – Stop conception by thickening cervical mucus
 c. Stage 3 – Stop implantation- by thinning the uterine wall

B. _RU 486 (First abortion pill)_

1. Synthetic steroid used 5-7 weeks after conception (First Trimester)
2. Deprives baby of vital nutritional hormone progesterone
3. Child starves to death as nutrient lining of the womb sloughs off
4. Mother delivers a child that has died.

C. __Dilation & Curettage__
   1. Used in the first trimester
   2. Dilate cervix to allow the insertion of curette – a loop-shaped knife – into the womb
   3. Instrument scrapes placenta from the uterus and cuts baby apart; pieces are drawn through the cervix

D. __Suction & Aspiration__
   1. Used in the first trimester
   2. Mouth of the cervix is dilated
   3. Hollow tube with knifelike edged tip is inserted into the womb.
   4. A suction machine with force 28 times greater than a vacuum cleaner literally rips the developing baby to pieces and sucks the remains into a container to be disposed.

E. __Dilation and Evacuation__
   1. Used between 12 and 24 weeks (primarily second trimester)
   2. The child is cut into pieces by a sharp knife, as in D & C.
   3. The child is much larger and far more developed.
   4. The child weighs as much as a pound and is as much as a foot in length.

F. __Prostaglandin__
   1. Used in the second trimester
   2. Prostaglandin hormones are injected into womb or released in a vaginal suppository which causes the uterus to contract and deliver baby prematurely.
   3. Sometimes a saline solution is used to kill baby before the premature birth

G. __Saline Injection__
   1. Used in the late second and third trimesters
   2. <u>Amniotic fluid</u> is removed and replaced with a toxic saline solution.
   3. Baby ingest the toxins and dies 1-2 hours later from salt poisoning, dehydration, and hemorrhaging.
   4. 24 hours later the mother goes into labor delivering a dead baby.
   5. Chemical burning of the skin causes a painful death for the baby.

H. __Hysterotomy__
   1. Used in the third trimester
   2. Baby removed as in a Cesarean birth
   3. Baby set aside and allowed to die or killed by a deliberate act.

I. __Dilation and Extraction D&X or Partial Birth__ (No longer legal in the U.S.)
   1. Used in late third trimester
   2. Guided by ultrasound, the abortionist grabs the baby's legs with forceps
   3. The baby's leg is pulled out into the birth canal
   4. The abortionist delivers the baby's body, except for the head

5. The abortionist jams scissors into the baby's skull. The scissors are then opened to enlarge the skull.
6. The scissors are removed, and a suction catheter is inserted. The child's brains are evacuated out, causing the skull to collapse. The dead baby is then removed.

IV. Arguments that support that a new life begins at conception.

A. Arguments from **SCIENCE**

[handwritten: Peter Singer - L mans -90 days can abort]

"Many people mistakenly feel that abortion is a "religious" issue. But it is not. It is a scientific issue, and specifically, a biological issue."
(http://www.johnankerberg.org/Articles/apologetics/AP0805W3.htm)

Dr. Keith L. Moore, Professor and Chairman of the Department of Anatomy, University of Toronto – Essentials of Human Embryology states: Human development is a continuous process that begins when an ovum from a female is fertilized by a sperm from a male. Growth and differentiation transform the zygote, a single cell… into a multicellular adult human being."

(Keith Moore and T.V.N. Persaud in The Developing Human (7th edition, 2003) *the most widely used textbook on human embryology)

Professor Micheline Matthews – Roth, Harvard University Medical School:

"In biology and in medicine, it is an accepted fact that the life of any individual organism, reproducing by sexual production, begins at conception."

(http://topics.nytimes.com/top/reference/timestopics/subjects/a/abortion/index.html?s=oldest&offset=70&inline=nyt-classifier)

B. Arguments from **Scripture (The Bible)**
1. The unborn are known by God. (Jeremiah 1:5; Psalm 139:13; Job 31:15)

2. The life of the unborn is protected by the same punishment for injury or death as that of an adult (Exodus 21:22-23)

3. Christ was human from the point of conception (Matthew 1:18; Luke 1:35)

4. Unborn children possess personal characteristics such as sin (Psalm 51:5) and joy (Luke 1:41, 44) that are distinctive of persons

5. The unborn are called by God before birth (Genesis 25:22-23; Judges 13:2-7; Isaiah 49:1)

6. Unborn babies are called "children" (Luke 1:41, 44, 2:12, 16; Exodus 21:22)

7. The same Greek word (*brephos*) is used for a baby inside the womb and outside the womb (Luke 1:41, 44-2:12,16; 18:15; Acts 7:19; II Timothy 3:15)

V. A HELPING STRATEGY: *The Woman Considering an Abortion*

> *Taken from: The Billy Graham Workers Handbook.*
> *A copy of the entire handbook can be downloaded free in a PDF from:*
> <http://theranch.org/fileadmin/_temp_/about/handbook/bgcwhandbook.pdf>

A. Commend her for calling.

B. Tactfully remind her that she quite possibly has strong feelings about the moral implications of abortion, or she wouldn't have called.

C. Avoid being judgmental about her situation.

D. Question her about her feelings on abortion:
   1. What promoted you to call about your problem?
   2. What are your real feelings about abortion?
   3. What have you heard from others, Christian or not regarding abortion?

E. Whether or not she believes abortion is wrong, present the Scriptures given in class along with any others that you think would apply.

F. Ask her to consider the alternatives.

G. If she is concerned about not being able to care for or support the child, ask her to consider adoption.

H. Ask her if she has ever received Jesus Christ as her Lord and Savior. If appropriate, present the gospel.

I. Suggest that she start reading the Bible.

J. Ask if she has a church home. She should try to identify with a Bible-teaching church where she can find fellowship and encouragement and can grow in her faith.

VI. The Woman Who Has Had an Abortion and Suffers from Guilt

A. Encourage her by saying that she has made the right choice in seeking help. We care and want to help in any way we can. God has an answer to every human situation, and she can trust Him to work for her good.

B. Don't make a moral issue of her situation; at the same time, don't minimize the seriousness of such a choice. The fact that she is willing to share her feelings of guilt is an indication that God is speaking to her.

C. Dwell on God's forgiveness for those who are willing to repent and confess their sins to the Lord. To the woman taken in the act of adultery, Jesus forgave her (John 8:11).

D. Should confession result, do not dwell on the past (Philippians 3: 13-14).

E. Ask if she has ever received Jesus Christ as her personal Savior. If appropriate, present the gospel.

F. Suggest that she seek fellowship with God through Bible reading and prayer. Forgiveness is immediate, but a sense of restoration and acceptance will come in due time. Through commitment to this important discipline of prayer and Bible study, she will grow in her relationship with God.

G. Suggest that she seek, or restore, fellowship with a Bible-teaching church. There she can counsel with a pastor, hear God's Word taught, and find strength through Christian relationships.

H. Pray with her. Ask God for forgiveness, commitment, and strength for the future.

VII. Selected Readings for Healing

A. **Anger**
   1. Ephesians 4:26, 31-32
   2. Hebrews 12:15

B. **Depression**
   1. Psalm 40:1-5, 8-17
   2. Psalm 6

C. **Forgiveness**
   1. Psalm 32:1-5
   2. Psalm 51:1-3
   3. I John 1:9
   4. II Corinthians 5:21
   5. Colossians 3:12-13

D. **Peace**
   1. Colossians 3:15
   2. Matthew 11:28-30
   3. Isaiah 26:3-4

E. **Support**
   1. Galatians 6:1-2
   2. Psalm 27

F. **Perseverance**
   1. Hebrews 12:1-2
   2. Galatians 2:20
   3. I Corinthians 6:11
   4. Philippians 3:13-14

Chapter 9: Euthanasia

Chapter Overview:

Admonition from Scripture

Euthanasia Etymology

Types of Euthanasia

Prominent Names to Know

Key Historical Cases

Five Main Arguments

Commonly Used Defenses for Euthanasia

Consequences

Traditional Arguments against Euthanasia

Biblical View

What Can We Do?

"Protecting from one end of the age spectrum to the other, we see euthanasia for the elderly as the counterpart to abortion for the very young. There is no moral distinction between the two. Quality-of-life proponent Joseph Fletcher agrees: 'To speak of living and dying, therefore... encompasses the abortion issue along with the euthanasia issue. They are ethically inseparable.' Those who take comfort in the fact that euthanasia is not practiced at present in America are leaning on a slim reed."

— Schaeffer, Francis, The Great Evangelical Disaster, Crossway, 1984

"These reasons for the importance of studying ethics all presume that there is such a thing as genuine moral knowledge. But that notion is being increasingly called into question in philosophy today as a result of the cultural dominance of the worldview of naturalism. Among other things, the naturalist holds that all reality is reducible to that which can be perceived with one's senses—that is, there is nothing that is real or that counts for knowledge that is not verifiable by the senses. As a result, moral knowledge has been reduced to the realm of belief and is considered parallel to religious beliefs, which the culture widely holds are not verifiable."

— Scott B. Rae, Moral Choices: An Introduction to Ethics

ADMONITION FROM SCRIPTURE

> **Deuteronomy 5:17 (NLT)** *"Do not murder"*

> **Job 1:21(NKJV)** *"And he said: 'Naked I came from my mother's womb, and naked shall I return there. The Lord gave, and the Lord has taken away; Blessed be the name of the Lord."*

> **II Corinthians 12:9 (NKJV)** *"And he said to me, 'My grace is sufficient for you, for My strength is made perfect in weakness.' Therefore, most gladly I will rather boast in my infirmities, that the power of Christ may rest upon me."*

I. Euthanasia Defined

The intentional killing by act or omission of a dependent human being for his or her alleged benefit. (The key word here is "intentional". If death is not intended, it is not an act of euthanasia)

II. Euthanasia Etymology

The term euthanasia is derived from the Greek prefix <u>eu</u>, meaning "____good____" or "____easy____", and the Greek nun <u>Thanatos</u>, meaning "____death____." Today the word is used to denote the act of one person killing another because the person killed is terminally ill, suffering, disabled, or elderly.

III. Euphemisms for Euthanasia

   A. "Death with Dignity"   C. "Compassion in Dying"   E. "Good Death"

   B. "Dying Gracefully"   D. "Planned Death"

IV. Types of Euthanasia

   A. ____Passive____ Euthanasia

   Withholding medical treatment or discontinuing treatment… "Letting die" …cause of death is the same as the condition causing the suffering (disease, respiratory failure, etc.)

   B. ____Active____ Euthanasia

   Actively doing something to bring about the death of the patient… lethal injection, smothering with a pillow, etc… the cause of death is not the condition causing the suffering, but rather something else.

C. _____Involuntary_____ Euthanasia

Patient does not request their own death – someone else decides for them that they are better off dead. This usually occurs when a patient is unable to communicate (coma) or unable to understand their condition.

D. _____Voluntary_____ Euthanasia

Patient requests their own death - either verbally, in writing or via a Living Will. (Some states will recognize testimony of family/friends, but not all.)

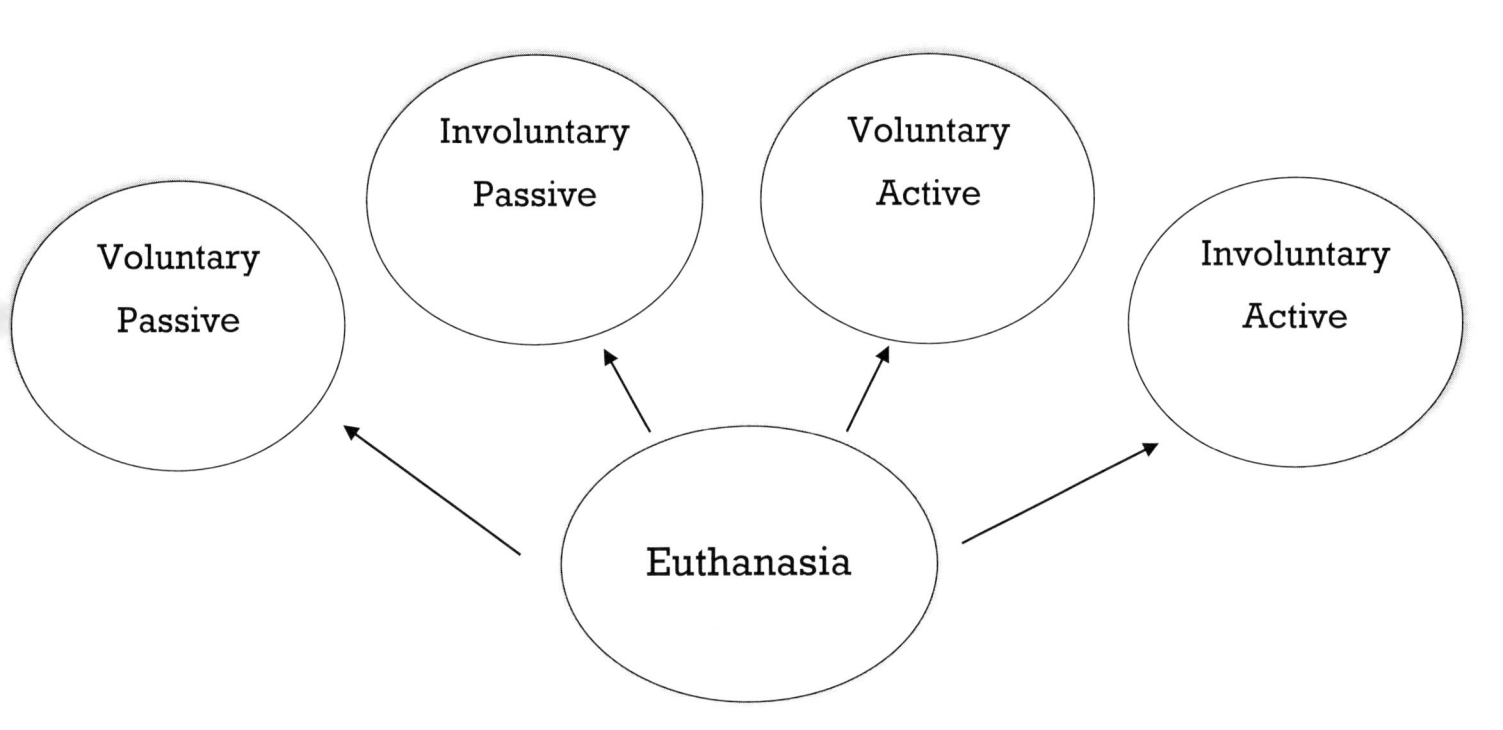

Euthanasia branches into four types:
- Voluntary Passive
- Involuntary Passive
- Voluntary Active
- Involuntary Active

These types combine to give us 4 Basic Forms of Euthanasia

Physician- Assisted Suicide

A person's reasons for dying are similar to that of euthanasia. However, rather than taking his or her own life, the person is assisted in the suicide by a physician.

Dr. Kevorkian

V. Prominent Names to Know and Key Events:

A. Derek Humphry

The head of Hemlock Society

B. Dr. Jack Kevorkian

Dr. Death

C. **Karen Ann Quinlan** – persistent vegetative state – They thought she would be the first euthanasia case and taken off life support in 1976. She lived 10 more years.
D. **Terry Schiavo** – suffered severe brain damage in 1990 and finally taken off life support and feeding tube in 2005 and died.
E. **Barbara Coombs Lee** – President of Compassion & Choices
F. **Brittany Maynard** – Advocate of Aid in Dying – January 1, 2014 was diagnosed with brain cancer. After treatment, the brain cancer returned in April 2014 and she was given six months to live. She moved to Oregon and on November 1, 2014 and ended her life (used Oregon's Death with Dignity Act)

VI. Key Historical Cases and Legislation

A. Baby Doe (Infanticide): April 1982
B. ___Nancy Cruzan___ : 1983-1990, Cruzan vs. Missouri *(did not know Nancy's wishes)*
C. Patient Self Determination Act: gave hospitals the responsibility to provide advanced directives.
D. Measure 16 and Death with dignity Act: Oregon's Assisted Suicide law – October 1997.
E. November 2008: Washington State became the second state to legalize Doctor Assisted Suicide.

VII. Five Main Arguments Used to Promote Euthanasia

A. Choice
B. Control
C. ___Compassion___
D. Cash
E. ___Capability___

VIII. Commonly Used Defenses for Euthanasia
   A. It is a __religious__ issue.
   B. Guidelines can prevent uses/abuses.
   C. It would only be for the "hard cases"
   D. We euthanize __animals__ to relieve suffering, why not people?
   E. There is no difference between "choice" in abortion and "choice" in euthanasia. Is this statement true or false?

IX. Consequences
   A. When life is devalued, it slowly depreciates further over time.

   "Protecting from one end of the age spectrum to the other, we see euthanasia for the elderly as the counterpart to abortion for the very young. There is no moral distinction between the two. Quality-of-life proponent Joseph Fletcher agrees: 'To speak of living and dying, therefore ... encompasses the abortion issue along with the euthanasia issue. They are ethically inseparable.' Those who take comfort in the fact that euthanasia is not practiced at present in America are leaning on a slim reed."
   (Schaeffer, Francis, The Great Evangelical Disaster, Crossway, 1984)

   B. __Quality of life__ ethic is replacing a __Sanctity of Life__ ethic.
   C. A __right__ to die with eventually be transformed into a __duty__ to die.
   D. The power to __choose__ will broaden from the individual to the "caregivers" to those "financially invested" to "institutions" and so on.
   E. Options will become less available.
   F. Expanding expendability inevitable.

X. Traditional Arguments against Euthanasia
   A. Expanding Expendability
   B. Physician/Patient relationship will weaken
   C. Quality of life ethic leads to come lives being deemed less worthy of life than others
   D. Abuses of the process & guidelines
   E. Diagnoses and prognoses may be __wrong__.
   F. There will become a __duty to die__.
   G. Violation of the __Hippocratic Oath__

XI. Biblical View of Euthanasia
   A. Man is created in the __image of God__ (Genesis 1:26)
   B. Human life is __sacred__ and should not be terminated merely because it is difficult.
   C. God is sovereign over life and death (Job 1:21; Deuteronomy 32:39; Psalm 139:16)
   D. The Bible specifically condemns the taking of life (Exodus 20:13)
   E. Our body as well as our spirit belongs to God (I Corinthians 6:19-20)
   F. God has a purpose for everything even when we don't understand that purpose
   G. (Romans 8:28; 11:33)
   H. Suffering has a place in God's __economy__ (2 Corinthians 1:8)
   I. As a result of the fall, __death__ is inevitable (Romans 5:12; 6:23)

XII. **What is** ___Hospice___?

 A. Help patients and families deal with the fear of the unknown.
 B. Help with pain control
 C. Thoughts of suicide and depression are dealt with
 D. They deal with the "burden" issue
 E. They help the family deal with the care of dying

XIII. **What Can We Do?**

 A. Be informed.
  1. Inform ___populace of alternatives___.
  2. Inform people of the dangers of "___cracking the door___".
  3. Medical schools need to train doctors in ___pain___ management.
 B. Be Involved.
 C. Be In Touch.

Chapter 10: Gender Issues

Chapter Overview:

Admonition from Scripture

Evangelical Responses

Men and Women in Society

Men and Women in the Home

Woman Serving in the NT

Gender Dysphoria & Transgender Movement

> *There is neither Jew nor Gentile, neither slave nor free, nor is there male and female, for you are all one in Christ Jesus.*
>
> The Apostle Paul – Galatians 3:27-28

> *"In contemporary parlance, sex is biological and gender is socially constructed."*
>
> Rebecca Solnit – The Mother of all Questions

> *"If women are expected to do the same work as men, we must teach them the same things."*
>
> Plato – The Republic

ADMONITION FROM SCRIPTURE

Proverbs 31:10 (KJV) *"Who can find a virtuous woman? For her price is far above rubies."* (Read the whole chapter)
Ephesians 5:24-25 (NLT) *"As the church submits to Christ, so wives must submit to your husbands in everything. And you husbands must love your wives with the same love Christ showed the Church."*
Acts 18:26 (KJV) *"And he (Apollos) began to speak boldly in the synagogue: whom when Aquila and Priscilla had heard; they took him unto them and expounded unto him the way of God more perfectly."*
Genesis 2:18, 20b-25 (NIV) *"The Lord God said, 'It is not good for the man to be alone. I will make a helper suitable for him.' But for Adam no suitable helper was found. So, the LORD God caused the man to fall into a deep sleep; and while he was sleeping, he took one of the man's ribs and then closed up the place with flesh. Then the LORD God made a woman from the rib he had taken out of man, and he brought her to the man. The man said. 'This is now bone of my bones and flesh of my flesh; she shall be called 'woman', for she was taken out of man.' That is why a man leaves his father and mother and is united to his wife, and they become one flesh. Adam and his wife were both naked, and they felt no shame."*

I. **Two Evangelical Responses to the Gender Debates:**

   A. **Egalitarianism (Biblical Feminism)** - the belief and interpretive framework that attempts to apply basic feminist ideas of equality to the scriptures and thus to the home and church. While rejecting the extremes of feminism, the tendency is to interpret scriptures as a "patriarchal" book limited to its time and culture. It focuses on the new ways in which women were being viewed and treated by Jesus and even suggested by Paul as totally equal to men in every way and not to be limited in terms of ministry opportunities by their gender.

   B. **Complementarianism** – a response to biblical feminism to reaffirm that men and women are equal in essence or identity having both been created in image of God, but still having different roles in the home and church. In the home, the man is to be the loving head of the woman, and the woman is to voluntarily submit to his leadership. In the church, God has ordained that men are to lead the church, and women are to support this work in the use of their gifts. There are God – ordained roles according to gender, and it is in fulfilling them that both women and men will find their greatest fulfillment in life.

II. Men and Women in Society

A. Both were created in the image of __God__ - Genesis 1:27
B. Both were to subdue and rule over everything on the earth – Genesis 1:28
C. Both could receive any of the spiritual __spiritual__. There are no gender distinctions – Romans 12; I Corinthians 12
D. Both could be business leaders in the community. – Proverbs 31:10 – 31
   1. There is NO reason why a woman cannot be a CEO etc…..
   2. There is NO reason why women shouldn't receive equal pay for equal work.

> Different roles are traced back to creation, not the fall of man. Leadership and submission have nothing to do with superiority and inferiority.

> "The principle of subordination and authority pervades the entire universe. Paul shows that woman's subordination to man is but a reflection of that greater general truth. Christ is the head of every man, and the man is the head of a woman, and God is the head of Christ. If Christ had not submitted to the will of God, redemption for mankind would have been impossible, and we would forever be doomed and lost. If individual human beings do not submit to Christ as Savior and Lord, they are still doomed and lost, because they reject God's gracious provision. And if women do not submit to men, then the family and society as a whole are disrupted and destroyed. Whether on a divine or human scale, subordination and authority are indispensable elements in God's order and plan."(MacArthur, John F., *1 Corinthians: The MacArthur New Testament Commentary*, (Chicago: Moody Press 1984.)

III. **Men and Women in the Home**

   A. The role of the husband
      1. Love his wife and ___sacrific___ for her. –Ephesians 5:25; Colossians 3:19
      2. Head of the wife. – Ephesians 5:23,24; Titus 2:5; I Corinthians 11:3
      3. Provide for his ___family___. I Timothy 5:8
      4. Honor and respect his wife. – I Peter 3:7
      5. Provide a positive environment for children. Colossians 3:21
   B. The role of the wife
      1. Submit to her husband, (not to men in general). – Ephesians 5:22 – 24; I Peter 3: 1-6, I Corinthians 11:3
      2. Be a ___helpmate___ to him – Genesis 2:18
      3. Love her husband and children. – Titus 2:4 Question: Why would God need to command this to wives?
      4. Keep the family a ___priority___. – Titus 2:5; I Timothy 5:14

IV. **How Women Served in the New Testament Church**

   A. Train younger women. – Titus 2: 3 -4
   B. Teach children. – II Timothy 1:5, 3:15
   C. Pray – I Corinthians 11:5
   D. Sing – Colossians 3:16 (Nothing gender specific. Note v. 18)
   E. Correct false teaching – Acts 18:26 (Aquila, Priscilla & Apollos)
   F. Vote – Acts 1:14-26 (Women took part in voting for a replacement for Judas Iscariot)
   G. Serve as Deaconess – Romans 16: 1,2 (Phoebe)

V. **Gender Dysphoria and the Transgender Movement**

   A. **Defining Terms**

   1. **LGBTQ** – lesbian, gay, bisexual, transgender, queer, or questioning.

   2. **Sexual Orientation** – It describes which gender identities a person is most attracted to sexually and/or romantically.

   3. **Transgender** - It is the "T" in LGBTQ. Some people have a gender identity that doesn't match up with their biological sex. For example, they were born with "female" sex organs (vulva, vagina, uterus), but they feel like a male. People in this community sometimes call themselves transgender or trans. (It is suggested not to use terms like

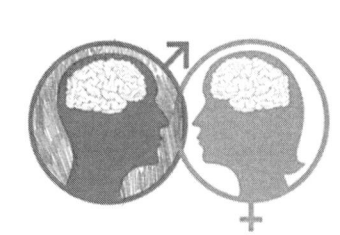

transgendered, tranny, or, he-she — they are considered old-fashioned and hurtful).
   a. It's used as the umbrella term for the transgender and transsexual community.
   b. Specifically defined as anyone whose gender expression (communication of gender) is considered non-traditional for the sex they were assigned at birth, such as transsexuals, cross dressers, drag artists, androgynous individuals, genderqueers, masculine women, feminine men and other gender variant individuals.

4. **Transsexual**
   a. A person who identifies psychologically as one gender/sex other than the one to which they were assigned at birth.

   b. To match their outer body to their inner sense of gender/sex, a transsexual person may change or have changed their body through hormone therapy and gender confirmation surgeries.

5. **Gender Dysphoria** - Gender dysphoria refers to deep and abiding discomfort over the incongruence between one's biological sex and one's psychological and emotional experience of gender.

6. **Intersexual** (Formerly known as Hermaphrodite)
   a. Many cases of intersexuality have their origin in utero and involve varying degrees of what is called Androgen Insensitivity Syndrome (AIS).
   b. This insensitivity to androgen – a male sex hormone – can interfere in the normal development of the sex organs and result in ambiguous genitalia as described above.
   http://www.pureintimacy.org/w/what-is-intersexuality-and-how-should-christians-respond/

B. Prominent names

1. **RuPaul Andre Charles** (born November 17, 1960), best known mononymously as RuPaul, is an American actor, drag queen, model, author, and recording artist. "When you become the image of your own imagination, it's the most powerful thing you could ever do." RuPaul (http://www.dragofficial.com/ali/25-rupaul-quotes-to-live-by)

2. **Bruce Jenner - Caitlyn Marie Jenner** ", formerly known as "Bruce Jenner", is an American television personality and retired Olympic gold medal-winning decathlete. On April 24th, 2015, in an interview with Dianne Sawyer, Jenner states, "Yes, for all intents and purposes I am a woman."

C. **How do we typically develop our male/female gender identity?**
  1. **Biological Influence**
     a. During fertilization, egg and sperm fuse, producing a cell with 46 chromosomes (22 pairs of autosomes and 1 pair of sex chromosomes)
     b. If the sperm that fertilizes the egg has an X chromosome, the embryo will be XX (female).
     c. If the sperm that fertilizes the egg has a Y chromosome, the embryo will be XY (male).
        ➢ Males and females have identical gonads (reproductive organs) until about 6 weeks after conception when SRY or DSS spur their development
        ➢ Once the testes or ovaries become functional their release of hormones controls further differentiation i.e. male and female sex organs.

D. **What can Influence Gender Dysphoria – Gender Problems at the Chromosomal Level?**
   a. Turner's syndrome – Female partially or completely missing an X chromosome – failure to begin sexual changes during puberty.
   b. Klinefelter's Syndrome – Anatomically male but results in sterility.
   c. Androgen Insensitivity Syndrome – Male with female genitals
   d. Fetally Androgenized Females – Female with male genitals
   e. DHT Lacking Males – Male appears as a female until puberty

E. **A Biblical Perspective on Gender Identity**

   1. **The Bible records God's creative order as seen in Male & Female.**

Genesis 1:26-27 (NIV) - *(26) "Then God said, 'Let us make human beings in our image, to be like us. They will reign over the fish in the sea, the birds in the sky, the livestock, all the wild animals on the earth, and the small animals that scurry along the ground.'(27) So God created human beings in his own image. In the image of God he created them; male and female he created them."*

Jesus addresses gender in Matthew 19:4 - *"Haven't you read," he replied, "that at the beginning the Creator 'made them male and female,'"*

   2. **Gender distinctions are obviously important to God** – Deuteronomy 22:5, Romans 1:24-25, 1 Corinthians 11:1-16.

   3. **Humans (Male & Female) are "broken" as a result of the Fall** (Genesis 3)

"The givenness of maleness and femaleness has of course been impacted by the fall, [...].

Thus, there are now on occasion gender anomalies in nature, and there is sometimes sexual confusion with the psyche of an individual. But anomalies and confusions in the fallen world do not negate the normative structure of God's designs. This givenness is the standard toward which we are to orient all sexual expression and the context in which all sexual behavior is to be experienced." Hollinger, (2009) The Meaning of Sex (p. 77)

Numerous passages emphasize the pervasiveness of our falleness/brokenness Genesis 6:5, 8:21, Psalm 51:5, Jer. 17:9, Romans 7:15-24 (but don't forget v. 25)!

4. **God has called the church to love our transgender neighbors. (Matthew 22:39)**

5. **God has called the church to evangelize/disciple the world.** (Matthew 28:19-20)

6. **God has called the Church to "Speak the truth in love" with our brothers and sisters in Christ (Ephesians 4:15).**

Chapter 11: Homosexuality

Chapter Overview:

Admonition from Scripture

What does the Bible Say?

Myths

Homosexual views of Bible Passages

A Christian Approach

"One of the most striking things about the New Testament teaching on homosexuality is that, right on the heels of the passages that condemn homosexual activity, there are, without exception, resounding affirmations of God's extravagant mercy and redemption. God condemns homosexual behavior and amazingly, profligately, at great cost to himself, lavishes his love on homosexual persons."

- Wesley Hill, Washed and Waiting: Reflections on Christian Faithfulness and Homosexuality

"As important as the question is – "What does the Bible really teach about homosexuality? – The first and more significant question is "What does the Bible teach about everything? Which means you can't start with Leviticus 18 or Romans 1. We have to start where the Bible starts: in the beginning."

- Kevin DeYoung, "What does the Bible really teach about Homosexuality?"

ADMONITION FROM SCRIPTURE

Leviticus 18:22 (NLT) *"Do not practice homosexuality; it is a detestable sin."*
I Corinthians 6:9-11(NET) *"Do you not know that the unrighteous will not inherit the kingdom of God? Do not be deceived! The sexually immoral, idolaters, adulterers, passive homosexual partners, practicing homosexuals, thieves, the greedy, the drunkards, the verbally abusive, and swindlers will not inherit the kingdom of God. Some of you once lived this way. But you were washed, you were sanctified, you were justified in the name of the Lord Jesus Christ and by the Spirit of our God."*
Romans 1:26-27 (KJV) *"For this cause God gave them up unto vile affections: for even their women did change the natural use into that which is against nature: And likewise also the men, leaving the natural use of the women, burned in their lust one toward another; men with men working that which is unseemly, and receiving in themselves that recompense of their error which was meet."*

I. Homosexuality: What Does the Bible Say?

A. Homosexuality was considered a sin in the days of the ___Patriarchs___.
   1. Genesis 18:20 "Their sin is very grievous"
   2. Genesis 19:1-12 Sodom and Gomorrah – Was the sin of Sodom and Gomorrah only homosexuality? No. See also Isaiah 1 and Ezekiel 16:49-50
   3. Jude 7

B. Homosexuality was considered a "capitol crime" in the ___Mosaic___ Law.
   1. Leviticus 18:22 "abomination" or "detestable"
   2. Leviticus 20:13
   3. Note: ___Moral laws and ceremonial laws___

C. The ___New Testament___ is clear in its condemnation of homosexual conduct.
   1. I Corinthians 6:9-10 (See above)
   2. Romans 1:24-32
   3. I Timothy 1:8-10 (NIV) "We know that the law is good if one uses it properly. We also know that the law is made not for the righteous but for the lawbreakers and rebels, the ungodly and sinful, the unholy and irreligious, for those who kill their fathers and mothers, for murderers, for the sexually immoral, for those practicing homosexuality, for slave traders and liars and perjurers – and for whatever else is contrary to the sound doctrine."

II. The Homosexual Agenda

A. Homosexuality qualifies for minority status and special legal protection.

> **Note:** The Civil Rights Act, which was passed in 1964, outlawed discrimination on the basis of color, race, religion, sex and national origin. Leaders within the gay rights movement have pushed for sexual orientation to be added to this list. General Colin Powell said, "Skin color is a benign, non-behavioral characteristic". He also stated that "Sexual orientation is perhaps the most profound of human behavioral characteristics. Comparison of the two, racial and sexual discrimination, is a convenient but invalid argument." Powell, Gen. Colin. The Retired Officer, July 1992.

The U.S. Supreme Court in various cases has determined minority status on the basis of three specific criteria. They are:

1. Economic Deprivation
   a. Gay couples have similar income levels as heterosexual couples, USA Today Report 11/03/2009
   b. Based upon the 2012 Lesbian, Gay, Bisexual, Transgendered, Demographic Report, individual/household income for lesbian gay women and homosexual men was greater than heterosexual individual/household incomes.

2. Political Powerlessness
   a. 1973 American Psychological Association removed homosexuality as a behavioral disorder.
   b. 1980 Democratic Party Platform adopted a plank in support of federal gay rights legislation.

3. Immutable (unchangeable) Characteristics
   a. Title VII of the Civil Rights Act of 1964 defines immutable characteristics as things like skin color, hair texture or certain facial features.

B. Homosexuals compose _____10%_____ of the U.S. population
1. Response: This figure was based on the now discredited Kinsey sex studies of 1948-1952. Even homosexual leaders have recognized this but still use it in their propaganda for recruitment.
2. Response: the 2010 U.S. Census indicated that there were 131,729 married same sex couples and 514,735 same-sex couples.
3. Response: In 2021, 7.1% of the U.S. population identify themselves as gay. This is up from 5.6 % in 2020. Gallup – February 2022 Report.

C. **Homosexuality is** _genetically_ **determined, thus uncontrollable.**
   1. Response: Although several studies have indicated that this may be the case, the fact still remains that there is no conclusive scientific evidence that this is true.
   2. Response: Converted homosexuals invariably say that this lifestyle they led was a personal choice. Even some homosexuals are not going for the genetic determinism argument.
   3. Response: Because of the sin nature in all human beings, there are internal and external influences which can impact human behavior. This does not mean that those influences determine human choice. Humans can make choices contrary to nature/nurture which if acted upon would, according to a Biblical/Christian worldview, be sinful.

D. **Homosexuals cannot** _change_.
   1. Response: There are too many former homosexuals who testify that they learned and then unlearned this behavior, while in it they were convinced they could not help themselves.
   2. Organizations for helping people change though the power of Christ. Organizations Ministering to Homosexuals.
      a. Homosexuals Anonymous (Germany)
      b. New Creation Ministries: www.newcreationministries.tv
      c. Regeneration (MD) 410-661-0284

III. Homosexual Views of Bible Passages
A. The sin of Sodom was not homosexuality but _inhospitality_. This is due to the interpretation of Yada. Genesis 19:5
B. Some believe David and Jonathan were gay lovers. I Samuel 18 -20; key verses 18:3-4; 20:41
C. I Corinthians 6:9 only speaks against offenses (i.e. improper homosexual activity).

IV. A Christian Approach to Homosexuality
A. SPEAK THE _Truth_ IN _LOVE_
   1. "speaking the truth in love" (Ephesians 4:15)
   2. "And a servant of the Lord must not quarrel but be gentle to all, able to teach, patient, in humility correcting those were are in opposition, if God perhaps will grant them repentance, so that they may know the truth, and that they may come to their senses and escape the snare of the devil, having been taken captive by him to do his will." (2 Timothy 2:24-26)

B. **HOMOSEXUALITY IS A** _Behavior_ **PATTERN THAT CAN BE** _changed_.

"Do not be deceived: Neither the sexually immoral nor idolaters not adulterer's not male prostitute's not homosexual offenders… will inherit the kingdom of God. And that

is what some of you were. But you were washed, you were sanctified, you were justified in the name of the Lord Jesus Christ and by the Spirit of our God."
(I Corinthians 6:9-11)

C. _____Help_____ **THOSE WHO WANT TO** _____Overcome_____ **Homosexuality.**

"Brethren, if a man is overtaken in any trespass, you who are spiritual restore such a one in a spirit of gentleness, considering yourself lest you also be tempted. Bear one another's burdens, and so fulfill the law of Christ." (Galatians 6:1-2)

FIGURE 1

Response: Homosexuality

Secondary cause: Sin

Primary cause: Biology or deficit in relationship with same-sex parent, low self-esteem, etc.

Common though unbiblical conceptualization of the development of homosexuality

FIGURE 2

Sinful practice: Homosexuality

Possible necessary influences: Genetics, peers, family, sexual violation by older person, etc.

Sufficient cause: sinful heart

Biblical conceptualization of the development of homosexuality

(Illustration from Welch, Edward. Homosexuality: Current Thinking and Biblical Guidelines. http://www.afa.net/homosexual_agenda/homosup.pdf)

D. **What should be My Attitude toward Homosexuality?**

(Taken from: *The Moral Catastrophe* by David Hocking)

1. Do not hate homosexuals; hate homosexuality and what it does to people.

2. Never believe that "sexual preferences" should be added to our understanding and application of human rights or civil rights.

3. Do not discriminate against homosexuals in terms of the rights to which all Americans are entitled, but never be intimidated or pressured to approve or accept their lifestyle and activity.

4. Teach your children what the Bible says about sexual matters, and warn them of sexual sins (adultery, homosexuality etc.)

5. Do not treat homosexuality as a more terrible sin than adultery among heterosexuals, but never view it as harmless or tolerable.

6. Encourage homosexuals to accept God's love and forgiveness in the work and person of Jesus Christ. Show them that God's power can give them the inner strength, courage, and desire not to be involved in homosexual activities.

7. Make sure that your own personal beliefs, principles and lifestyle are in line with biblical morality. You should be committed to demonstrating that the only safe and right sex is between a husband and a wife.

Chapter 12: Relationships: Biblical Principles & Guidelines

Chapter Overview:

Admonition from Scripture

Three Biggest Decisions

Dating Define

Types of Dating

Purpose of Dating

Seven Habits

Pitfalls of Dating

Before Saying "I Do"

Biblical Principles to Apply

10 Ways to Practice Purity

10 Principles for Christian Dating That Will Transform Lives.

-Frank Paul

1. Stop looking for "the one"
2. Date with a trajectory towards marriage.
3. Don't date non-Christians
4. Don't "flirt to convert"
5. Have a list of values and don't compromise them
6. Don't "shotgun" date
7. It's ok to WANT to get married. It's also ok NOT to get married.
8. Have a community of Christians around you… and LISTEN to them.
9. Pursue a pure mind.
10. Don't date if you are dependent on someone for things only God can provide.

ADMONITION FROM SCRIPTURE

II Corinthians 6:14-15 (TLB) *"Do not be teamed with those who do not love the Lord, for what do the people of God have in common with the people of sin? How can light live with darkness? ... How can a Christian be a partnered with one who doesn't believe?"*

I Thessalonians 4:3-5 (NIV) *"It is God's will that you should be sanctified: that you should avoid sexual immorality; that each of you should learn to control your own body in a way that is holy and honorable, not in passionate lust like the pagans, who do not know God."*

II Timothy 2:22 (TLB) *"Run from anything that gives you the evil thoughts that young men often have but stay close to anything that makes you want to do right. Have faith and love and enjoy the companionship of those who love the Lord and have pure hearts."*

The Three Biggest Decisions of Your Life

1. Who is my __Master__?
2. What is my __Mission__?
3. Who is my __Mate__?

I. Dating Defined
A prearranged social activity shared by two single persons of the opposite sex. (Group dating involves several couples enjoying a similar activity together.)

II. Types of Dating
A. Recreational or casual dating involves a relationship that revolves around an event. There is no commitment beyond a date.
B. Attachment-oriented dating or serious dating involves some level of commitment. Dating revolves around their relationship rather than the event.

III. Purpose of Dating
A. __Achieving Status__ (This is not a positive purpose)
B. Recreation – Just to have a good time
C. To learn more about the opposite sex and how to behave toward them.
D. It enables one to learn more about oneself.
E. It is preparatory socialization for marriage and family roles.
F. To help a person choose their spouse.

IV. **Seven Habits of Highly Defective Dating.**
   A. Dating leads to intimacy but not necessarily to __commitment__.
   B. Dating tends to skip the "__friendship__" stage of a relationship.
   C. Dating often mistakes a physical relationship for __love__.
   D. Dating often __isolates__ a couple from other vital relationships.
   E. Dating, in many cases, distracts young adults from their primary responsibility of preparing for the future.
   F. Dating can cause discontentment with God's gift of singleness. (a string of uncommitted relationships is not a gift.)
   G. Dating creates an artificial environment for evaluating another person's __character__ (Note: while the above 7 CAN be true, it DOES NOT have to be that way)

V. **Pitfalls of Dating**
   A. When the physical aspect is dominant, the social, intellectual, and __spiritual__ elements of the relationship will suffer.
   B. The possibility of getting to serious too fast (Friendship, Dating, Relationship, Engagement, Marriage)
   C. Reputation – Proverbs 22:1
   D. Flesh Control – James 1:14-17 Lust (Ephesians 2:1-3) & Modesty (I Timothy 2:9)
   E. How far is too far? – Is it?
      1. All the way (I Corinthians 6:9-11)
      2. When it becomes lust (I Thessalonians 4:4-9)
      3. When one feels guilty (Romans 14:13-23)
      4. Comparing is impairing.

Where will you draw the line?

No Physical Contact
Holding Hands
Kissing
Passionate Kissing
Caressing, Fondling, Oral Sex
Sexual Intercourse

VI. Three Important Steps before Saying "I Do".

A. Recognize the danger signals in dating.
1. Fighting
2. Breaking up Frequently
3. _serious doubts_
4. Desire to date others
5. Depression/Moodiness
6. Extreme difference in _Friendships_
7. Physical/emotional abuse
8. Length of acquaintance
9. Desire to marry in spite of the warnings

B. Determine if you really love them. Take the "Love Test".
1. _Spiritual_ Consideration _2 Cor. 6:14-18_
2. Intelligence and Ability _____
3. Common Interests _____
4. Similarity of _____
5. Attitude or philosophy of life (worldview) _____

C. Analyze the six factors of compatibility during engagement to determine if you should get married.
1. Spiritual _____
2. Financial _____
3. Parenthood _____
4. Relatives _____
5. Social Activities _____
6. Friends and Associates _____

VII. Biblical Principles to Apply when Dating

A. What kind of person should you date?
II Timothy 2:22, TLB. *"Run from anything that gives you the evil thoughts that young men often have, but stay close to anything that makes you want to do right. Have faith and love, and enjoy the companionship of those who love the Lord and have pure hearts."*

B. Don't date someone who doesn't love God.
II Corinthians 6:14-15, TLB. *"Don't be teamed with those who do not love the Lord, for what do the people of God have in common with the people of sin? How can light live with darkness? … How can a Christian be a partner with one who doesn't believe?"* Amos 3:3 *"Can two walk together, unless they are agreed?"*

C. **Don't date someone who claims to be a Christian but doesn't live it.**

I Corinthians 5:11, TLB. *"What I meant was that you are not to keep company with anyone who claims to be a brother Christian but indulges in sexual sins, or is greedy, or is a swindler, or worships idols, or is a drunkard, or abusive."*

D. **Inner beauty counts the most.**

I Peter 3:4, TLB. *"Be beautiful inside, in your hearts, with the lasting charm of a gentle and quiet spirit that is so precious to God."*

E. **In a dating relationship don't be exclusive--care about others too.**

Philippians 2:4, TLB. *"Don't just think about your own affairs, but be interested in others, too, and in what they are doing."*

F. **Let the relationship progress step by step.**

I Peter 1:6-7, TLB. *"Next, learn to put aside your own desires so that you will become patient and godly, gladly letting God have his way with you. This will make possible the next step, which is for you to enjoy other people and to like them, and finally you will grow to love them deeply."*

G. **What to avoid on dates.**

Romans 13:13, TLB. *"Be decent and true in everything you do so that all can approve your behavior. Don't spend your time in wild parties and getting drunk or in adultery and lust, or fighting, or jealousy."*

H. **Dating should not include a sexual relationship.**

I Corinthians 6:13, 18, TLB. *"But sexual sin is never right: our bodies were not made for that, but for the Lord. . .That is why I say to run from sex sin. No other sin affects the body as this one does. When you sin this sin it is against your own body."*

I Thessalonians 4:3-5, TLB. *"For God wants you to be holy and pure and to keep clear of all sexual sin so that each of you will marry in holiness and honor--not in lustful passion as the heathen do, in their ignorance of God and his ways."*

(Taken from: www.bibleinfo.com)

VIII. **10 Ways to Practice Purity** (Campus Life – Jan/Feb 2001)

A. Keep innocent expressions innocent.
   (Rather than making innocent expressions a mere prelude to "heavier stuff.")
B. Pace your Passion
   (Realize you are trying to remain pure all the way to your wedding day)
C. Don't feed fantasies.
   (Feeding your thought life with junk only makes it harder to remain pure.)
D. Remember whose property you're touching.
   (That person belongs to God)

E. Make a promise to God, and daily renew your commitment. (Seek God and draw the line, then keep it.)
F. Acknowledge Jesus' presence on every date.
   (Start & finish your date with prayer)
G. Agree on your standards.
   (Talk about your standards/line together)
H. Don't always go it alone.
   (Be selective where and spend time with others)
I. Put real love first. (Always respects)
J. Declare a new beginning. (Start Now)

Chapter 13: Racism

Chapter Overview:

Admonition from Scripture

Racism Defined

How is Racism Manifested

What is Racism Based On?

Biblical Response

Key Issues for the Church

Combat with Biblical Truth

"Hating people because of their color is wrong. And it doesn't matter which color does the hating. It's just plain wrong." – Muhammed Ali

"I refuse to accept the view that mankind is so tragically bound to the starless midnight of racism and war that the bright daybreak of peace and brotherhood can never become a reality…I believe that unarmed truth and unconditional love will have the final word." – Dr. Martin Luther King, Jr.

"Then Peter began to speak: "I now realize how true it is that God does not show favoritism but accepts men from every nation who fear Him and do what is right." (Acts 10:34-35 NIV)

"The Christian belief that God created all humans in His image (Genesis 1:26-27) must guide all decision-making regarding people. Everyone has intrinsic value. God loves everyone and so should all Christians. We should love them enough to share the truth of God's Word and the hope it provides." – Dr. Lew Weider

ADMONITION FROM SCRIPTURE

> **II Corinthians 12:13 (TLB)** *"Some of us are Jews, some are Gentiles, some are slaves, and some are free. But we have all been baptized into Christ's body by one Spirit, and we have all received the same Spirit."*
>
> **Galatians 3:28 (TLB)** *"There is no longer Jew or Gentile, slave or free, male or female. For you are all Christians – you are one in Christ Jesus."*
>
> **Acts 17:26 (KJV)** *"And has made of one blood all nations of men for to dwell on all the face of the earth."*
>
> **John 3:16 (NKJV)** *"For God so loved the world that He gave His only begotten Son, that whoever believes in Him should not perish but have everlasting life."*

I. **Racism Defined:** The belief that certain racial distinctions determine human value.

   Note: Racism is an individual belief, not simply a cultural or institutional belief.

II. **How is Racism Manifested?**

   A. **Stereotyping** – A (usually negative) overgeneralization about a certain people group as a whole based on the unaccepted behavior of a few members of that group.

   B. **Prejudice** – "Prejudging" an individual in a negative way because he/she happens to be from a stereotyped group.

   C. **Discrimination** – Unequal treatment of a person on the basis of his/her people group membership.

   D. **Hate speech/crimes** – Verbal and physical abuse directed toward people. This is considered justified because of their group membership.

   E. **Genocide** – Deliberate and systematic killing of an entire race or ethnic group, usually based on the belief that ones being killed are evil or inferior and have no legal right to life.

Jackson loves Jesus

III. **What is Racism Based on?**
   A. _Irrational Beliefs_ - That a certain people group as whole is intellectually or morally inferior
   B. _Pride_ - Especially in inherited traits and culture
   (See I Corinthians 4:7)
   C. _Ignorance_
      1. Educational
   "the evolutionary view that life can evolve to 'higher' levels provides fuel for racist ideas. The Bible on the other hand, clearly shows the fallacy of racism... this misleading concept gives rise to the idea that some "races" have developed and become more sophisticated faster than others, leading to the ultimate conclusion (often subconsciously) that certain 'races' are superior"
   (Creation Ex Nihilo 20 Dec 97)
      2. Voluntary – I choose to have racist attitudes etc.
   D. _Fear_
      1. Of unknown
      2. Of what is different
   E. _Socialization_
      1. Parental example
      2. Uncritically accepted social assumptions

Acts 17:26 (KJV) "And has made of one blood all nations of men for to dwell on all the face of the earth."

Illustration used by permission from "Answers in Genesis"

IV. **Biblical Response to Racism**
   A. **As believers, we are all one** _in Christ_.
   Galatians 3:28 (TLB) "We are no longer Jews or Greeks or slaves or free men or even merely men or women, but we are all the same – we are Christians; we are one in Christ Jesus."

   B. **Racism** _is a sin_.
   James 2:8-9 (NIV) "If you keep the royal law found in Scripture, 'Love your neighbor as yourself,' you are doing right. But if you show favoritism, you sin and are convicted by the law as lawbreakers."

C. All men have the same __blood__.

Acts 17:26 KJV "And has made of one blood all nations of men for to dwell on all the face of the earth."

D. **God accepts people from** __every race__, __culture__, **and** __religion__.

Acts 10:34 – 35 NIV "Then Peter began to speak: ' I now realize how true it is that God does not show favoritism but accepts men from every nation who fear Him and do what is right.'"

V. Key Issues for the Church

A. Interracial Marriage

1. Marry __believers__ - 1 Corinthians 7:39.
2. What is a __mixed__ marriage? - Deuteronomy 7:3-4; Exodus 12:48-49; 2 Corinthians 6:14; Colossians 3:9-11.
3. What are some questions to ask?
   - What are your cultural differences?
   - What do your families think about the marriage?
   - What are the consequences for your children?
4. Notice Numbers 12:1, 10.
5. *What does the Bible say about the problems of interracial marriages?* __Nothing.__

B. Racial __unity__ among believers

1. Why do believers of different races struggle to be in the same church together?
2. There are cultural differences, but they must not be practiced at the expense of unity.
3. Obstacles that block progress *(from Tony Evans – Can We Really Get Along? – an article taken from his book Let's Get to Know Each Other)*
   - Our fear of losing our racial distinction
   - Our cultural prejudice
   - Our fear of the price tag of unity
   - Our hesitancy to hold people accountable for racial prejudice
4. Jesus' example in John 4.
5. Our priority - John 13:34-35; Luke 10:30-37; James 2:1-13.

VI. Combating Racism with Biblical Truth

A. **Abrahamic** _____ – Genesis 12:1-3, 15:5-6; Romans 4:17-18; Galatians 3:26-29

B. **The Curse of Ham?** Genesis 9:18, 26; 10:6, 15-19

http://www.answersingenesis.org/Home/Area/AnswersBook/races18.asp

C. **Mosaic** _____ – Exodus 23:9

D. **Jesus'** _____ – John 4:1-10 (The Samaritan Women at the well)

E. **Jesus'** _____ – Luke 10:25-37 (Parable of the Good Samaritan)

F. **The _____ breaks down divisive barriers and unifies races**
   - Acts 15:7-9; Romans 1:14-16; I Corinthians 12:13; Galatians 3:28; Ephesians 2:13-20; Colossians 3:10-15

G. **Heaven will be a _____ celebration of Christ.**
   – Revelation 5:9-10

Chapter 14: Poverty

Chapter Overview:

Admonition from Scripture

Biblical View of Wealth

4 Causes of Poverty

Reasons for Poverty

Biblical Observations on Poverty

Minister to the Poor

Christian Attitude

10 Principles

Make a Difference

"There are people in the world so hungry, that God cannot appear to them except in the form of bread." –Mahatma Gandhi

We are not rich by what we possess but by what we can do without." – Immanuel Kant

"Anyone wanting to proclaim the glory of Christ to the ends of the earth must consider not only how to declare the gospel verbally but also how to demonstrate the gospel visibly in a world where so many are urgently hungry." - David Platt

"God's definition of what matters is pretty straightforward. He measures our lives by how we love." –Francis Chan

ADMONITION FROM SCRIPTURE

> **Proverbs 14: 20,31 (NKJV) (20)** *"He who despises his neighbor sins; but he who has mercy on the poor, happy is he. (31) He who oppresses the poor reproaches his Maker, but her who honors Him has mercy on the needy."*

> **Matthew 25:35-36 (NIV)** *"For I was hungry and you gave me something to eat, I was thirsty and you gave me something to drink, I was a stranger and you invited me in, I needed clothes and you clothed me, I was sick and you looked after me, I was in prison and you came to visit me."*

> **Galatians 2:10 (NLT)** *"The only think they suggested was that we remember to help the poor, and I have certainly been eager to do that."*

I. A Biblical View of Wealth

A. Wealth is not Condemned
   Genesis 13:2 (Abraham); Deuteronomy 8:28; Proverbs 22:2

B. When wealthy people in the Bible were condemned, it was because of the Means by which they obtained their wealth.
   (Amos 4:11; 5:11)

C. Christians should be concerned about the effect that riches can have on our lives.
   1. We may no longer look to God and even forget Him. (Proverbs 30:8-9; Hosea 13:6)
   2. Pride – (Proverbs 28:11; Jeremiah 9:2)

II. Four General Causes of Poverty

(Taken from "Wealth and Poverty" – Kerby Anderson. www.probe.org)

A. __Oppression__ & Fraud (Individuals, Governments) Proverbs 14:31; 22:7; 28:17; James 5:1-4

B. __Misfortune__ - __Persecution__, or Judgment Job 1:12-19; Psalm 109:16; Lamentations 5:3)

C. __Laziness__, Neglect, Gluttony Proverbs 10:4; 13:4; 19:15; 20:13; 23:21)

D. __Culture__ of Poverty

   "Poverty breeds poverty and the cycle is not easily broken" – Kerby Anderson
   Proverbs 10:15 "The ruin of the poor is their poverty

Understanding of Poverty:
What does it mean to be poor?

Category	%
Lack of food	47%
Lack of money	35%
Lack of employment	23%
Lack of shelter	22%
Lack of clothing	17%
Low living standards	16%
Lack of everything	8%
Low levels of health	8%
Lack of education	6%
No cattle or livestock	6%

www.usaid.gov/.../images/photos/surveys-3.jpg

III. Reasons for Poverty

Many different factors have been cited to explain why poverty occurs. No single explanation has gained universal acceptance. Factors that have been alleged to cause poverty include:

A. State discrimination and corruption. Abuse of public power.
B. Lack of social integration.
C. Crime.
D. Substance abuse
E. Procrastination
F. Natural factors such as climate or environment.
G. War, including civil war, genocide and democide.
H. Lack of education and skills.
I. Individual beliefs, actions and choices.

Facts on Poverty in the United States

- Adults not working – 29%
- Adults without a high school diploma – 25%
- Adults with a disability – 25%
- Single Moms – 23%
- Black Americans – 20%
- Hispanic Americans – 21%
- Foreign Born non-citizen's – 18%
- All Children – 16%
- Single Fathers – 11%
- Seniors – 9%
- Married Couples – 5%
- Adults with college degrees or higher – 4%
- Full time working adults -2%

U.S. Poverty Statistics released September 2021 by the U.S. Census Bureau

2020-2021 Federal Poverty Guidelines (Contental United States)

Household Size	100% FPL Annual Gross	150% FPL Annual Gross	200% FPL Annual Gross	300% FPL Annual Gross
1	$12,760	$18,140	$25,520	$38,280
2	$17,240	$25,860	$34,480	$51,720
3	$21,720	$32,580	$43,440	$65,160
4	$26,200	$39,300	$52,400	$78,600
5	$30,680	$46,020	$61,360	$92,040
6	$35,160	$52,740	$70,320	$105,480
7	$39,640	$59,460	$79,280	$158,560
8	$44,120	$66,180	$88,240	$176,480

MedicarePlanFinder.com
Powered by MEDICARE Health Benefits

IV. Biblical Observations on Poverty
A. Poverty is __perpetual__.
(Deuteronomy 15:11; Matthew 26:11; Mark 14:7; John 12:8)
B. Poverty may be consequences of sinful __personal choices__. (but not always.
(Proverbs 10:4; 19:15)
C. Poverty may be a consequence of sinful choices __made by others__.
(but not always) (James 5: 1-4)
D. Poverty is not __shameful__
Jesus was poor – Matthew 8:20; 2 Corinthians 8:9
God may have a purpose for the poor – James 2:5

V. Biblical Reasons Why Christians Should Minister to the Poor.
A. God __expects__ it – Deuteronomy 15:11; Leviticus 19:10; I John 3:17

B. Paul's example - Galatians 2:10

C. The principle of __sowing and reaping__ - Galatians 6:7-10; Matthew 5:7

D. God will reward those who give - Proverbs 19:17; 22:9; 28:27

E. When Christians give to the poor they are giving to__-Matthew 25:31-46

VI. A Christian Attitude toward the Poor
A. Consider others __better__ than ourselves – Philippians 2:3; I Corinthians 10:24
B. We are not to be a respecter of persons - James 2:1-9
C. We are to love our __neighbors__ as ourselves - Matthew 22:39
D. The Golden Rule - Matthew 7:12; Luke 6:31
E. When you see a __need__, meet it if you can. - James 4:17; Luke 10 25-37

VII. Ten Principles to Govern Giving Assistance to the Poor through an Organization.

A. – Does the program demand accountability from the people it serves?

B. – Does the program stress the building of character? "Give a man a fish and feed him for a day. Teach him how to fish and feed him for a lifetime"

C. – Do the providers use judgment to give help on an individual basis?

D. – Does the program require work of those who can work? (II Thessalonians 3:10)

E. – Does the program teach recipients how to free themselves from their dependent status?

F. – Does the program foster true self-esteem by leading them to their creator and His principles?

G. – Does the program have a success rate that can be quantified?

H. – Does the program conduct periodic assessment to determine its effectiveness?

I. – How much money donated goes directly to the poor?

J. – Are volunteers utilized to keep cost down and to provide a meaningful ministry for people.

Programs that help the poor are intended to be a "safety net" not a "hammock".

VIII. Ten Suggested Activities to Make a Difference.

A. Volunteer at a soup kitchen

B. Open a food pantry and clothing center in the church

C. Tutor students and adults

D. Provide basic job training

E. Provide child care services for single parents or others who are in real need

F. Be a mentor to children from broken homes

G. Help with Habitat for Humanity

H. Work with urban shelters for the homeless

I. Clean up parks and recreational facilities to provide good activities for kids and families

J. Become informed about the specific needs of your community

CONCLUSION

➢ Yes, we feed their bodies but more importantly we must feed them spiritually. Not just bread made by hand but the Bread of Life. (Jesus). (Isaiah 61:1; Matthew 11:5)

For further readings to consider:
1. Capitalism and Freedom by Milton Freidman
2. Free to Choose by Milton Freidman
3. Race and Culture: A World View by Thomas Sowell
4. Poverty and Wealth by Ronald Nash
5. Social Justice and the Christian Church by Ronald Nash
6. Biblical Economics Manifesto by Gill and Nash
7. The Road to Serfdom by F.A. Hayek

Biblical Worldview and Contemporary Issues Resource List

Beckwith, Francis J., and Gregory Koukl. *Relativism: Feet Firmly Planted in Mid-Air.* Grand Rapids: Baker Press, 2001.

Beckwith, Francis J., William Lane Craig, and J. P. Moreland, eds. *To Everyone An Answer: A Case for the Christian Worldview.* Downers Grove, Illinois: InterVarsity Press, 2004.

Beilby, James K. *Thinking About Christian Apologetics.* Downers Grove, Illinois: IVP Academic, 2011.

Benedict, Ruth. *Patterns of Culture.* 1934. Boston: Houghton Mifflin Company, 1989.

Bertrand, J. Mark. *(Re)Thinking Worldview: Learning to Think, Live, and Speak in This World.* Wheaton: Crossway Books, 2007.

Bruce, Tammy. *The Death of Right and Wrong.* Roseville, California: Prima Publishing, 2003.

Budziszewski, J. *Written On The Heart: The Case For Natural Law.* Downers Grove, Illinois: InterVarsity Press, 1997.

Chaffee, John. *Thinking Critically.* 6th ed. Boston: Houghton Mifflin Company, 2000.

Colson, Charles., and Nancy Pearcey. *How Shall We Then Live.* Wheaton: Tyndale House Publishers, 1999.

Copan, Paul and William Lane Craig, eds. *Contending With Christianity's Critics.* Nashville: B&H Academic, 2009.

Copan, Paul. *That's Just Your Interpretation: Responding To Skeptics Who Challenge Your Faith.* Grand Rapids: Baker Books, 2001.

_____. *When God Goes To Starbucks: A Guide To Everyday Apologetics.* Grand Rapids: Baker Books, 2008.

Coppenger, Mark. *Moral Apologetics for Contemporary Christians.* Nashville, Tennessee: B&H Publishing Group, 2011.

Corduan, Winfried. *Pocket Guide to World Religions.* Downers Grove, Illinois: InterVarsity Press, 2006.

Craig, William Lane and Chad Meister. *God is Good God is Great: Why Believing in God is Reasonable and Responsible.* Downers Grove, Illinois: IVP Books, 2009.

Craig, William Lane. *Reasonable Faith: Christian Truth and Apologetics*. Wheaton, Illinois: Crossway Books, 2008.

Dawkins, Richard. *The God Delusion*. New York: Houghton Mifflin Company, 2006.

Dembski, William A. *The End of Christianity: Finding A Good God in an Evil World*. Nashville: B&H Publishing Group, 2009.

Dembski, William A. and Michael R. Licona, eds. *Evidence for God*. Grand Rapids: Baker Books, 2010.

Dockery, David S., ed. *Faith and Learning: A Handbook for Christian Higher Education*. Nashville, Tennessee: B&H Academic, 2012.

Dockery, David S and Timothy George, eds. *The Great Tradition of Christian Thinking: A Student's Guide*. Wheaton, Illinois: Crossway, 2012.

Fletcher, Joseph. *Situation Ethics*. Philadelphia: Westminster Press, 1966.

Gilbert, Greg. *What Is The Gospel?*. Wheaton, Illinois: Crossway, 2010.

Goheen, Michael, W. and Craig G. Bartholomew. *Living At The Crossroads: An Introduction to Christian Worldview*. Grand Rapids: Baker Academic, 2008.

Groothuis, Douglas. *Truth Decay: Defending Christianity Against the Challenges of Postmodernism*. Downers Grove, Illinois: InterVarsity Press, 2000.

_____. *Christian Apologetics: A Comprehensive Case for Biblical Faith*. Downers Grove, Illinois: IVP Academic, 2011.

Harris, Sam. *Letter to a Christian Nation*. New York: Vintage Books 2006.

Haught, John F. *God and the New Atheism: A Critical Response to Dawkins, Harris, and Hitchens*. Louisville: Westminster John Knox Press, 2008.

Hexham, Irving. *Understanding World Religions*. Grand Rapids: Zondervan, 2011.

Hibbs, Thomas S. *Shows About Nothing: Nihilism in Popular Culture from the Exorcist to Seinfeld*. Dallas: Spence Publishing Company, 1999.

Hiebert, Paul G. *Transforming Worldviews: An Anthropological Understanding of How People Change*. Grand Rapids: Baker Academic, 2008.

Hoffecker, W. Andrew, ed. *Revolutions in Worldview: Understanding the Flow of Western Thought*. Phillipsburg, New Jersey: P&R Publishing, 2007.

Holmes, Arthur F. *Ethics: Approaching Moral Decisions*. Downers Grove, Illinois: IVP Academic, 2007.

Horner, David A. Mind Your Faith. Downers Grove, Illinois: IVP Academic, 2011.

House, H. Wayne and Dennis W. Jowers. *Reasons for Our Hope: An Introduction to Christian Apologetics*. Nashville, Tennessee: B&H Academic, 2011.

Huffman, Douglas S., ed. *Christian Contours: How a Biblical Worldview Shapes the Mind and Heart*. Grand Rapids, Michigan: Kregel Publications, 2011.

Keller, Timothy. *The Reason for God: Belief in an Age of Skepticism*. New York: Dutton, 2008.

Luther, Martin. Harold Grimm, ed. *Christian Liberty*. Philadelphia, PA: Fortress Press, 1957.

MacArthur, John. *Think Biblically: Recovering a Christian Worldview*. Wheaton, Illinois: Crossway Books, 2003.

Markos, Louis. *Apologetics for the 21st Century*. Wheaton, Illinois: Crossway, 2010.

McDowell, Josh. *The New Evidence That Demands A Verdict*. Nashville: Thomas Nelson, 1999.

McDowell, Josh and Bob Hostetler. *The New Tolerance: How a Cultural Movement Threatens to Destroy You, Your Faith, and Your Children*. Wheaton, Illinois: Tyndale House Publishers, 1998.

Mohler, R. Albert Jr. *Atheism Remix: A Christian Confronts the New Atheists*. Wheaton, Illinois: Crossway Books, 2008.

_____. *Culture Shift, Engaging Current Issues with Timeless Truth*. Colorado Springs, Colorado, Multnomah Books, 2008.

Moreland, J. P. *Love Your God with All Your Mind: The Role of Reason in the Life of the Soul*. Colorado Springs: NavPress, 1997.

Moreland, J. P. and William Lane Craig. *Philosophical Foundations for a Christian Worldview*. Downers Grove, Illinois: InterVarsity Press, 2003.

Morrow, Jonathan. *Think Christianly: Looking at the Intersection of Faith and Culture*. Grand Rapids, Michigan: Zondervan, 2011.

Noebel, David, A. *Understanding The Times*. Manitou Springs, Colorado: Summit Press, 2008.

Paul, Richard W. and Linda Elder. *Critical Thinking: Tools for Taking Charge of Your Professional and Personal Life.* Upper Saddle, New Jersey: Financial Times Prentice Hall, 2002.

Pearcey, Nancy. *Saving Leonardo: A Call to Resist the Secular Assault on Mind, Morals, and Meaning.* Nashville: B & H Publishing Group, 2010.

_____. *Total Truth: Liberating Christianity from Its Cultural Captivity.* Wheaton, Illinois: Crossway Books, 2004.

Piper, John and David Mathis, eds. *Thinking, Loving, Doing: A Call to Glorify God with Heart and Mind.* Wheaton, Illinois: Crossway, 2011.

Samples, Kenneth Richard. *A World of Difference: Putting Christian Truth-Claims to the Worldview Test.* Grand Rapids: Baker Books, 2007.

Sire, James W. *The Universe Next Door.* Downers Grove: Intervarsity Press, 5th edition, 2009.

Sproul, R. C. *The Consequences of Ideas: Understanding the Concepts That Shaped Our World.* Wheaton, Illinois: Crossway Books, 2000.

Stetson, Brad and Joseph G. Conti. *The Truth About Tolerance: Pluralism, Diversity and the Culture Wars.* Downers Grove, Illinois: InterVarsity Press, 2005.

Walsh, Brian J. & J. Richard Middleton. *The Transforming Vision: Shaping a Christian Worldview.* Downers Grove: Intervarsity Press, 1984.

Waxman, Trevin. *Counterfeit Gospels: Rediscovering the Good News in a World of False Hope.* Chicago, Illinois: Moody Publishers, 2011.

Weider, Lew and Ben Gutierrez. *Consider.* Virginia Beach, Virginia: Academx Publishing Services, 2011.

Wells, David F. *The Courage to be Protestant: Truth-lovers, Marketers, and Emergents in the Postmodern* World. Grand Rapids, Michigan: William B. Eerdmans, 2008.